HELP!

My Dog Won't Sleep

Toni Shelbourne
&
Karen Bush

ISBN: 9798367928969

ACKNOWLEDGMENTS

Thanks to the following who generously supplied photographs – sorry we couldn't use them all!
Caroline Wilkinson, Charlotte Bull, Clare Grierson, Cressida Staddon, Dawn Cassar, Hannah Lockwood, Julie Payne, Kellyann Cottrell-Easton, Liz Kirtley, Lizi Arnold, Mandy Cottrell, Marie Hannon, Megan Myers, Natalie Finch, Rachael Landymore, Rebecca Hanlon, Ruth Haynes, Sally Tribe.

For simplicity, throughout this book, dogs have been referred to as 'he'

Disclaimer

CONTENTS

Introduction   7

1
The importance of sleep   9

2
Sleep deprivation   23

3
Getting a good night's sleep   41

4
Puppies   89

5
Beds   99

6
A little extra help   117

Further Reading   137

Useful contacts & resources   139

About the authors   152

INTRODUCTION

We invest a lot of time, effort and money on food, toys, grooming, and vet bills; we strive to ensure our dogs have sufficient exercise, enrichment and plenty of attention from us − but one of the most important essentials for making sure your pet has a happy and healthy life is often overlooked.

Sleep is absolutely key to good physical and mental health; it can also play a vital part in the bond between you and your dog, and in the success of your training. By understanding your dog's sleep patterns, knowing what's 'normal' and what isn't, and how you can promote the restful slumber that they need, you can ensure they enjoy life as a healthy and happy part of your family.

1
THE IMPORTANCE OF SLEEP

Sleep affects almost every single type of tissue and system in the body – from the brain, heart and lungs, to immune function, disease resistance and metabolism.

It also plays an important role in mood, memory and learning processes; your dog is not 'doing nothing' while slumbering, as memories are being consolidated and emotional balance restored. In one study, dogs who slept well after being taught a new action, performed better than those who didn't when tested on it again a week later.

Housekeeping is another essential function; metabolic waste products and toxins that build up in the brain while awake are removed faster and more efficiently while sleeping than waking.

• Impaired sleep has also been associated with Alzheimer's disease, a condition which dogs can suffer from, as well as humans. Studies suggest that sleep plays a part in clearing beta-amyloid from the brain, and that sleep deprivation can lead to a build-up of it. Beta-amyloid is a toxic metabolic waste product found in the fluid between brain cells; in Alzheimer's disease it clumps together to form plaques which hinder communication between neurons.

• Good quality sleep plays a crucial role in supporting the immune system, and enables a more efficient response to vaccines; research in humans has shown that the immune response is weaker if the recipient has had a poor night's sleep following a vaccination, and there is no reason to suppose that dogs are any different in this respect.

Types of sleep
Humans are 'monophasic' sleepers, receiving our sleep in one extended time period of around 6-8 hours. Dogs on the other hand, are 'polyphasic' sleepers, meaning that they sleep in multiple periods throughout a 24-hour cycle, with the enviable ability to sleep anywhere, any time. Their sleep can be restorative whilst sleeping during the day as well as at night, whereas humans don't get the full benefits which night time sleep provides.

Dogs do, however, have similar sleep cycles to humans, although they are shorter, so that where a human will go through 4-5 cycles a night on average, a dog will experience 15-20 cycles during a 24-hour period. During each sleep cycle, both humans and dogs progress through similar stages:

Stage 1 – light, dozing sleep, easily awoken, muscles still active and ready for action.

Stage 2 – blood pressure, heart rate, breathing and body temperatures gradually lower.

Stage 3 – hard to wake up as sleep deepens and awareness of the outside world fades before transitioning into REM sleep.

Stage 4 - Rapid Eye Movement sleep (REM); the body becomes relaxed, but the brain remains active.

When Stage 4 finishes, your dog may wake up fully, or just partially; he may change position and will then start all over again at Stage 1.

Rapid Eye Movement (REM) sleep is the state associated with vivid dreams (see below, *Do dogs dream?*) During REM there may be muscle twitching, vocalisation, and if you look closely, you can observe rapid eye movements behind the closed eyelids. Unlike humans, dogs are able to move more swiftly through the first three stages of Short Wave Sleep (SWS) to REM sleep; some can enter this stage in under 20 minutes, but will stay in it for shorter periods, typically from 2 -6 minutes.

Each human sleep cycle lasts around 70-120 minutes, during which we cycle through these stages several times, with the REM cycles growing longer as the night goes on. Dogs however, have much shorter sleep cycles lasting only 45 minutes, during which they cycle twice through non-REM and REM sleep.

How much sleep?

On average a healthy adult dog may sleep in total anywhere between 7.7-16 hours in each 24 hour period with the average working out at around 10.1 hours. Just as with humans though, requirements can vary between individuals, and both puppies and seniors tend to need more rest.

At the neo-natal stage puppies may sleep for as much as 18-20 hours in each 24 hour period; this gradually diminishes and by the time a puppy has reached 16 weeks old he'll be sleeping for a total of around 11 hours in each 24 hour cycle. While many puppies sleep less at night than adult dogs, they generally sleep more during the day.

These daytime naps are just as important for your puppy as his night-time sleep, so make sure he gets quiet times to snooze undisturbed during daylight hours, especially if you have a busy household. Just like toddlers, an over-tired puppy who is not getting enough sleep can become cranky, resulting in increased biting/mouthing behaviour, hyperactivity, and a decreased ability to settle. Keeping your puppy awake during the day will not result in him sleeping through the night, you will just end up with unwanted behaviours.

As they become elderly, most dogs will also generally begin to sleep longer, although conditions such as Canine Cognitive Dysfunction may sometimes interfere with sleep patterns. Many larger breed dogs will also often sleep more than smaller ones.

Daily routine

When, and how long a dog may sleep will also depend on the level of activity in his day-to-day life. Working dogs such as sheepdogs, police and patrol dogs have lots of physical and mental stimulation which keeps them active and awake while pet dogs may be dozing at home to pass the time. Although little research has been conducted on the relationship between sleep and exercise in dogs, regular exercise does appear to help them sleep better. One study did however, observe that dogs who have the opportunity to sleep during the day are more relaxed and appear happier – so it is a case of achieving a good balance between activity and leisure time.

Like us, dogs process their day and deal with their experiences and emotions during sleep. Those who have had negative experiences in the day appear to have more trouble sleeping, or to sleep for a shorter time afterwards.

Too much sleep

While it's normal for most dogs to spend a lot of time either sleeping or dozing, sometimes it may change from being normal to being excessive. Signs to watch out for include lethargy (if your dog seems to generally lack energy while awake, as well as sleeping more) and other changes in his usual habits or health, such as appetite, thirst and toileting. Many dogs are creatures of habit, so changes in routine may sometimes be responsible, affecting your dog's normal sleep patterns. And just like humans, dogs can be subject to emotional and psychological turmoil and can become depressed, leading to them seeking refuge in extended periods of sleep.

As with humans, dogs are of course all individuals and may vary in how much they sleep from day to day, but if you do feel it is both excessive and persistent, your vet should be your first port of call as it may be related to various health issues. Incorrect nutritional levels in the diet, as well as hydration can also be contributory factors, and another point to discuss with your vet. Keeping a diary noting periods of sleep, plus any other indications that things aren't quite right can be helpful.

• It is possible to accurately keep track of how much and when your dog is sleeping, even if you aren't present by using a 'smart collar'. These are non-invasive, and depending on how sophisticated the product you choose is, can monitor a range of additional physiological and behavioural parameters such as pulse, respiration, calories consumed and burned, and movement. If your dog is experiencing sleeping problems, these devices may be worth investigating to help you in determining possible causes and to help provide your vet with more data.

Do dogs dream?
Since we can't actually ask our dogs, it's necessary to draw conclusions from available research, and this does point towards them dreaming, just as we do; they have similar brainwave patterns.

Although dreaming occurs during other

stages of sleep, it is during REM sleep that human dreams are most intense and are more likely to be memorable on waking. You'll often notice your dog's muscles and paws twitching, his tail wagging, and maybe hear him vocalise during the REM stage of sleep; the opinion of most scientists is that dreaming is the brain's way of processing information, through replaying past events.

Studies have demonstrated that there is activity during REM sleep in the same areas of the brain that are active when a dog is chasing prey, so it may be that he is reliving the day's activities, whether chasing a ball, a squirrel, playing with a friend or interacting with you.

Just as REM dreaming sleep decreases with age in humans, so this is mirrored in dogs. Puppies appear to spend more time in REM sleep than adult dogs, which may be because they have huge quantities of newly acquired experiences to process.

Not all dreams may be happy ones though. Just as people who are stressed and anxious may have frightening dreams, it's quite probable that this also applies to dogs.

Just as being deprived of REM sleep can cause unpleasant effects in humans, it's likely that the same applies to canines.

It's therefore important to allow your dog to sleep deeply when he wants to, and not to disturb him when he starts showing signs of dreaming.

Do not disturb!

The old adage 'let sleeping dogs lie' may be a metaphor, but it's one that should be taken quite literally too. Dogs who are sleeping deeply may also sometimes be disoriented on waking if their slumber is suddenly disturbed, causing them to strike out in panic as the startle response is triggered. It may occur in any age, size or breed of dog, although it's often seen in ex-racing greyhounds, street dogs and those from puppy farms who may have lacked early socialisation, had little contact with people and/or are unaccustomed to living in a home environment. If it really is necessary to wake your dog for some reason you should therefore take care and avoid actually touching him. Call his name instead while keeping a safe distance away; if he is deaf or becoming hard of hearing place a strongly scented treat near his nose instead. Be patient, as elderly dogs may take more time to rouse and become fully alert.

Only approach your dog when you're sure he's definitely awake; bear in mind that some dogs sleep with their eyes partially open.

Common Sleeping Positions

Your dog's sleeping position can reflect his mood, and may be influenced by emotional and psychological factors, as well as by physical pain and illness.

Above: 'Roaching' position
(Image©Toni Shelborne)

- **Curling up, nose to tail:** this position is often adopted by wild animals; it protects internal organs, conserves heat, and enables your dog to get up again quickly.
- **Lying on his side, exposing his belly:** dogs which feel entirely relaxed, at ease and secure in their surroundings will often lie like this, and it's often a position adopted when tired, and for deep sleep.
- **Lying on his back:** this is a familiar sight to many dog guardians – often with one or more paws in the air - and known as 'roaching'. Only dogs feeling very safe are likely to sleep like this, as it is a very vulnerable position. Exposing the belly to the air can also help with cooling down.
- **Lying on his chest:** Usually a restful position which allows your dog to relax, but he is more likely to be napping than drifting off into deep sleep.

How your dog positions himself relative to you or other dogs can also reveal how comfortable he feels in company: for example, an anxious dog is more likely to sleep in a position which makes it easier to leap to his feet and make a quick escape. However, the most important thing of all is to be aware of changes in sleeping position – for example, if a dog which formerly liked to curl up no longer does, or sleeps on his chest rather than on his side. It may indicate the onset of a health issue, and is certainly something to be investigated.

Above: Be alert to changes in sleeping position, or of preferences in surface or location, which might be indicative of a health issue.
(Image©Caroline Wilkinson)

Location, Location, Location

Location as well as body position can tell you a lot about your dog's state of mind. Fearful dogs may choose to sleep in a semi-hidden location: crates, behind sofas or in smaller places where they can protect their backs can often be preferred as a safe area in which to sleep.

Dogs who are napping, but want to be aware of what is going on around them so they don't miss out on any fun activities, generally nap in high traffic areas such as stairways, places where they can see out of windows, in the middle of rooms, or near to their people. Many dogs, come the evening, will take themselves off to their comfy bed (or yours) to settle down for the night.

Above: Dogs who don't like to miss out on anything may nap in high traffic areas.
(Image©Caroline Wilkinson)

2
SLEEP DEPRIVATION

Lack of sleep can be a serious issue; in addition to becoming grumpy and irritable, insufficient sleep can adversely affect long term health, increasing stress levels and impairing the body's own healing abilities.

It may not be immediately obvious that a dog is sleep-deprived, as initially he may be restless and hyperactive rather than seeming sleepy. But if allowed to progress, co-ordination, concentration and memory become affected, and he will be less able to cope with stressful stimuli. Behaviour may become unpredictable, with nervousness and irritability possibly leading to aggression.

Causes
It's not just your dog who will suffer the consequences of sleep deprivation: if he is waking at night and disturbing the household it will affect all the human occupants too. While he may be able to catch up on some of his rest during the day, taking a daytime nap, although beneficial, isn't quite as restorative (or always feasible to fit into a workday schedule) for his

human guardian as a regular good night's sleep.

The problem may be quite straightforward and easy to fix once you work out the root cause. The most common ones are:

I'm young:

Puppies just separated from their mothers and siblings may never have been alone, not for a single second. At this age it is extremely scary and stressful to be isolated; in fact you can set up a lifetime of anxiety trying to make a puppy sleep on his own. You'll find more information on how to help your new puppy get a good night's sleep in Chapter 4.

Dogs have a different circadian rhythm to us, which means their sleep patterns differ from ours. They are most active at dawn and dusk, so an adolescent dog is most likely to be awake and ready to go at these times. While dogs can and do learn to adapt to our cycle, it can take a while, so be patient and try to encourage a later start to the day by adding on just a few minutes at a time before you get up.

I'm old:

If your senior dog is waking you, he may need to toilet more often or be suffering from ill health or cognitive decline – Canine Cognitive Dysfunction (CCD), sometimes called 'doggy

Alzheimers' is often associated with sleep disturbances. Seek veterinary advice if his sleep patterns change.

I'm cold:

This is a common problem in the colder months. We think that our dogs will be fine; they have a fur coat, right? But many dogs suffer from being cold, young dogs, old dogs, and short, single-coated dogs included. Most households turn off, or at least turn down, the heating during the night; if your dog is regularly waking you during the coldest part of the night, usually around 3am, he is probably needing more warmth.

Think carefully about where you position his bed and the type of bedding you supply (see Chapter 5). Get down on the floor and notice how much colder it is at ground level, or if his bed is in a draught. Raising it off the ground, supplying him with extra blankets, or moving the bed to a warmer part of the house, can help.

I'm lonely:

Dogs are social animals; they thrive on company. If you go out to work, have children to ferry around to activities, or have a hobby your dog can't participate in, your dog could be spending too much time alone. Add in the eight hours you disappear to sleep, and you may realise your dog is being deprived of meaningful time spent in your company.

Think of ways he can spend more time with you, or work out a way he can sleep in the same room. He doesn't need to be on your bed, but being in the same room can make all the difference to his mental well-being.

I'm hungry:

As humans, we often choose what time our dog eats, and it's often more to do with our own convenience and not always when they wish to be fed. Many young, growing dogs can get very hungry during the night, and being hungry can really disrupt sleep. Young dogs may need more filling, slow-burning food to prevent hunger pangs.

It's not only growing adolescents who may suffer from night-time hunger-pangs, but dogs of all ages; try either slowly moving his evening meal to later or feed a small meal just before bedtime. At the opposite extreme, if some diets don't provide enough for your dog's needs, others may provide an excess, and some foods and additives may cause hyperactivity. Talk to a pet nutritionist for advice if you think that disrupted sleep patterns may be due to what he is eating.

Another common mistake is feeding your dog first thing in the morning so if he wakes up early he then shouts for his breakfast. This is often reinforced by guardians getting up and producing the meal – a cycle has begun. Break that expectation of a feed first thing in the morning, and after a short period, his early morning habit should settle.

I hurt:

Lack of sleep can make dogs more sensitive to pain; it can also be the reason for sleep disturbances. Older dogs with arthritis, or dogs with pain-related issues can often suffer at night. If he has a known painful condition, or if your senior dog is waking at night and is generally looking stiff in his movement, consult your vet. Seeking veterinary and alternative therapies, and changing his routine and management can help him feel more comfortable, so he is less likely to wake frequently at night.

I'm frightened:

Anxious dogs, puppies, dogs who have had a scare, dogs who suffer from separation anxiety: all may struggle to sleep alone. You can often tell if he is worried as his anxiety will heighten when he picks up on the cues to your own bedtime; he may be reluctant to enter the room you want him to sleep in, or become frantic and vocal.

It may not be your preference, but consider

your dog's emotional wellbeing if he is fearful. Studies show that it is just as beneficial for us as it is for our dogs to sleep together, so if your own sleep is being disturbed at night by your dog, it may be worth biting the bullet and trying having him in your bedroom (see Chapter 5).

I'm being disturbed:

Many things can disturb or arouse a dog at night. They don't sleep for a solid eight hours as we do; their shorter sleep/wake cycle means they will naturally have periods at night when they will wake. You may be surprised at how awake and active your dog is for much of the night.

They are also very light sleepers, and may be wakened even from deep sleep, by disturbances which may include:

● External security lights can be absolutely dazzling: it's not just the brightness which can be disturbing, but also the suddenness with which they come on and then go off again which can be disturbing. If you have an external light which comes on periodically throughout the night, it can wake your dog. If you have a dog you might not need an outside light anyway, as he will alert you to any trespassers, so turning it off can really aid sleep. However you will have no control over a neighbour's light, or you may need your own to remain on for some reason; in this case try fitting a good blackout blind or curtains, or putting your dog in a different room to sleep.

• Wildlife can be another issue; even if you don't have motion-activated external security lights for them to trigger. Dogs will wake at the slightest noise or movement. They can also be territorial, so if they have access to a window that overlooks the garden and he sees a wild animal or cat in his space, he is only doing his job by alerting you to the intruder. However, it's arousing and upsetting for him, and will make it harder for him to get back to deep sleep again after any alarm.
Blocking access to the window or shutting him out of that room may help. You could also try using white noise to mask external sounds.

• Noises can also be frightening for many dogs, whether fireworks, people outside in the street, even branches knocking against the windows.
    You'll need to try and work out what sound he may be hearing, and see if you can eliminate it; if it isn't possible, try a more distant room, masking the sound with white noise, and

hanging acoustic curtains to dampen sounds from outside. If thunder or fireworks are the problem, and your dog is really fearful, it's best if he is close to you, so you may have to let him sleep in the same room, even if it is only temporarily.

• Stormy or windy weather can be just as unsettling; garden furniture being blown around, branches tapping on windows and so forth can be very worrying. Your dog might be so frightened that for a time after the storm he may be unsettled at night; after a scary experience some dogs may even need to have their sleeping area relocated.

If you are trying to work out what is disturbing him, set up a night vision camera to monitor his behaviour.

• Some medications may also affect your dog's sleep, causing him to either sleep less or to sleep more and be generally more drowsy. Check with your vet if you think it may be related to changes in sleep patterns. Although not a common occurrence, products commonly used around Firework Night which contain Valerian and aim to promote a calming and soporific effect can sometimes have the opposite effect on a few individuals.

Daytime naps

Especially if your dog lives in a busy household, he may not be receiving all the sleep that he needs. Depriving your dog of REM sleep by constantly disturbing him interferes with his learning ability and memory, and can cause unpleasant physical effects. If you take your dog to a day care facility while you are at work, check as to what provision is made for quiet 'nap time' during the day.

Make sure children (and non-doggy visitors) are taught to leave the dog alone when in his own bed and never to wake him when asleep, wherever that is – both for safety and to ensure he is not constantly being disturbed. Just because your dog seems quite amiable about being woken for a game or even excited about it, doesn't mean that disturbing his sleep is either right or justified. Whenever he wakes up is time enough for some interaction.

• No matter how well run they are, some dogs may also find boarding kennels and rescue centres a stressful environment, with the noise and visitors as well as general anxiety at the strange new environment all contributing to poor quality or lack of sleep. Do not be surprised if when, on bringing him home he spends a lot of time sleeping – he may be catching up.

Sleep disorders
Sleep disorders do exist in dogs, although thankfully, they are in the main, uncommon. Where they are present, they may be responsible for periods of wakefulness at night, and your dog not getting enough of the right sort of rest. Sleep disorders include:

Sleep apnoea: It's not unusual for some dogs to snore gently while sleeping, but if it starts becoming louder, take notice as it may be an indicator of the onset of sleep apnoea. This occurs when the breathing suddenly stops, jolting the dog awake for 10-20 seconds at a time as breathing resumes again. Some dogs may have as many as 100 such breathing interruptions during the course of a single night, which they may or may not, be aware of. These frequent interruptions to sleep can leave the dog feeling tired and lethargic during the day, and more seriously, in severe cases can put him at increased risk of health issues such as heart disease, diabetes and stroke. The problem is most common in overweight dogs, and in brachycephalic (flat-faced) breeds such as English Bulldogs, Boston Terriers and Pugs, whose facial structure affects their airways. In some cases, the problem can be due to either seasonal or environmental allergens such as pollen and dust mites.

A visit to the vet will help determine the cause and best way of resolving it. If overweight, a special diet and exercise regime may need to be tailored to your dog: in the case of suspected allergens, an allergy test may be conducted, and medications prescribed. If the issue is due to abnormal anatomy, surgery may be the only option

Insomnia: Difficulty in going to sleep can be a canine problem as well as a human one, and can also be due to anxiety, stress and/or pent-up energy. However, very often it is due to physical issues including pain from an injury, or from arthritis; itchiness from skin conditions; gastric discomfort; or from a need to get up to toilet. Observation and a veterinary health check will help you to identify physical causes and determine the appropriate course of action.

Where anxiety and stress may be underpinning the issue, it will be helpful to ask an animal behaviourist for assistance, as it isn't always easy to spot stressors yourself.

For some dogs, it is more due to a desire to get up and get on with the day, particularly if it is a habit which starts at first light rather than persisting through the night. Black-out blinds may help keep the sun out, fooling your dog into thinking it is still dark; young dogs who haven't yet adapted to human sleeping habits will eventually grow out of it.

Bear in mind that as well as sleeping less, sleeping more can also be indicative of a health problem and should be checked out.

Canine Cognitive Dysfunction: Canine Cognitive Dysfunction (CCD) is a disease caused by brain changes in ageing dogs, which is similar to Alzheimer's in humans – it is also often referred to as 'doggy dementia' and 'doggy Alzheimer's'

There may be a variety of symptoms including disorientation, wandering aimlessly, changes in interaction with family members, irritability, forgetting training cues and behaviours, fearfulness, changes in appetite and activity, staring into space, and toileting indoors. A change in sleep patterns is a common symptom; a dog which is affected may begin sleeping more during the day and less at night when he may wander around, sometimes barking, and often becoming trapped in corners or by furniture.

CCD cannot be cured, and will continue to progress. Do seek help from your vet if your dog displays any of the symptoms associated with CCD, and bear in mind that many of them can be due to other health issues. If CCD is diagnosed, there are prescription drugs as well as dietary supplements which may be beneficial, with some appearing to slow down progression of the disease. It can be a challenging and emotional journey at times, but you will find that there are many publications and online groups which offer support as well as practical suggestions on living with a CCD dog.

REM behaviour disorder: It's perfectly normal for a dog's paws to twitch or tail to wag while he's dreaming, but paralysis of the large muscles during sleep keeps them from actually getting up and acting out those dreams. Dogs who suffer from this sleep disorder, where that paralysis is not enforced, will get up and walk round, and in extreme cases, it may cause them to run into walls or attack inanimate objects around them.

If you suspect this problem, consult your vet, who on diagnosis will be able to prescribe medication which will reduce symptoms and allow your companion to have a restful and safe night's sleep.

Narcolepsy: Usually affecting young dogs, narcolepsy is due to low levels of hypocretin, a hormone which plays an important role in regulating sleep and arousal states. Most commonly it is due to a genetic disorder affecting breeds including Dobermann Pinschers, Poodles, Dachshunds and Labrador Retrievers, but other causes include obesity, inactivity, immune system dysfunction – and sometimes the cause is simply unknown.

A dog with this condition will suddenly collapse and fall asleep, often triggered by a period of excitement or physical activity such as playing, eating, greeting visitors or family members. The muscles go slack and the dog appears to be in deep REM sleep. This may last from several seconds to 30 minutes after which he will wake abruptly, and continue as though nothing has happened. He may also come out of an episode in response to you talking or petting him. Sometimes a dog affected by narcolepsy will also have cataplexy which is similar, except that during an episode the eyes remain open and he has control over their movement, and the dog remains aware and conscious of what is going on around him.

Narcolepsy is incurable, but not painful or life threatening, but should be diagnosed by a vet – if you are able, try to video an incident which you can show him. Physical and neurological examination and laboratory tests will help to rule out other medical conditions.

Depending on severity and frequency of episodes, medication may be prescribed. You can also try as far as possible, to minimise those triggers which are identified as setting it off; for example, if he becomes excited by the arrival of visitors you can stay by his side and calm him with quiet words and gentle physical contact. Similarly, avoid areas such as dog parks where there may be many people and other dogs which might overstimulate him. As well as watching out for possible triggers, be aware of dangers in the terrain when on walks which might be hazardous in the event of an episode – near water or cliffsides for example – and put him on the leash. If necessary, there are many secure enclosed dog exercise areas which you can hire for a small fee, where your dog can run and play safely off leash.

Be ready to step in and protect him from

other dogs when an episode occurs, as sometimes it can provoke an aggressive reaction, even from a normally gentle and friendly canine friend.

Seasonal Affective Disorder: It's thought that dogs, as well as humans, can be affected by Seasonal Affective Disorder (SAD), a type of depression which is linked to the change in seasons. As daylight decreases, the brain produces more of the hormone melatonin and less serotonin, which can affect mood and activity levels. Little research has been conducted on the disorder, however, although a survey conducted by the People's Dispensary for Sick Animals (PDSA) indicated that many owners felt their dogs became lethargic and inclined to sleep more during the winter months.

Because the survey was subjective rather than scientific though, it's possible that the results were due more to the dogs involved mirroring their owner's reduced activity and inclination to take as much exercise and engage with their pets as during those months when the weather is warmer and days longer. If your dog is receiving adequate exercise and mental stimulation but is showing any of the signs of

SAD, including sleeping for longer periods, you should consult your vet in case there is a health issue at the root of it.

• Any change in sleeping habits should always be noted, along with changes in sleeping position. Sometimes changes are dramatic, but they can also creep in more slowly and go unnoticed at first.

If your dog suddenly starts to sleep for longer or shorter periods, or experiences disturbances in his sleeping pattern ask your vet to check him over so that if nothing else, you can at least eliminate any potential health issues as being the cause.

3
GETTING A GOOD NIGHT'S SLEEP

Ensuring your dog gets sufficient quality as well as quantity of sleep is an important part of keeping him happy and healthy as well as ensuring that your own sleep is not being disturbed every night. There are several strategies which you can adopt that you may find helpful.

Create the right environment

There are many things which can contribute to a good or bad night's sleep; creating the right environment is a factor which is often overlooked.

Light

Melatonin is often referred to as the 'sleep hormone' because it plays a central role in regulating the body's wake/sleep cycle. Synthesized and secreted by the pineal gland in the brain and released into the bloodstream it induces restfulness and sleep; however, this only takes place at night, when it gets dark. As it grows light again, the brain prompts the pineal gland to decrease the production of melatonin, resulting in waking up. Consequently, the sleep/wake cycle is synchronized with night and day, resulting in consistent and restorative sleep.

These days, light pollution, both indoors and outside, has become part and parcel of modern living, but if it affects melatonin production, will have an adverse effect on sleeping patterns.

External security lights with sensors which flick on and off all night with every little disturbance outside can also disturb your dog's sleep, so either switch them off, change the room he sleeps in or fit really good blackout curtains or blinds, but remember to secure any cords high up out of reach so there is no danger of your dog becoming entangled. Hanging blackout curtains at windows will help eliminate bright street lighting or moonlight, and the shadows they may cast, as well as views of nocturnal wildlife being seen through low windows. A bonus is that they can help fool super-early risers into thinking it's still night time outside, encouraging them to go back to sleep again.

Consider also the room in which your dog sleeps; if in the kitchen or utility room, are there electrical appliances illuminating the room? If they can't be turned off, move your dog's bed to a different location.

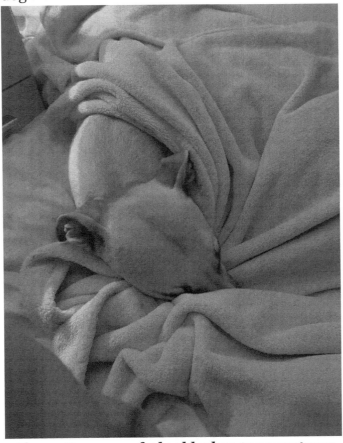

Above: Dogs may feel cold when temperatures drop, and may appreciate a cosy blanket.
(Image©Toni Shelbourne)

Temperature

Sleep quality can be affected by the ambient

room temperature; both being too warm or feeling cold will make for a restless night.

Factors you might not have considered – such as underfloor heating, or a bed being situated in a draught may create issues in maintaining a comfortable body temperature. Although your dog may have a favourite sleeping place, ensure that he can move to a different cooler or warmer area or room if he wishes. Because your dog's core body temperature is regulated by the circadian rhythm, rising during the day and dropping at night, feeling cold is often an issue during winter months when heating is turned down or off at bedtime. You'll find suggestions for helping your dog stay warm in Chapter 5.

Noise

Not only do we live – and expect our dogs to do so also – in a brightly lit world, but a noisy one too. The cacophony of sound which assaults us on a daily basis can easily overload your dog's nervous system, reducing the quality of his rest. Although the degree of sensitivity can vary between individuals and often declines with age, generally most dogs have far more sensitive hearing than us. They can hear at roughly four times the distance that humans can, and are able to detect much higher

44

frequency noises, such as those produced by 'silent' dog whistles and sonic noise deterrents. While you may think that everything is quiet at night, it's seldom the case; as well as the hum of household appliances, there are noises made by cooling radiators and the creaks that some houses make as temperatures drop at night. Outside, there may be the sound of passing pedestrians and traffic to disturb your dog, the slam of a car door, cats battling over territory, or of wildlife out and about, or there may simply be a twiggy branch which rattles unpredictably against a windowpane as breezes move it. Many sounds which might go unnoticed against the daytime backdrop of activity tend to become more noticeable at night.

Try and reduce or eliminate those noises which are within your control, turning off appliances where possible rather than leaving them on standby, remove any jingly tags and bells from collars, and don't turn on dishwashers and washing machines overnight.

Acoustic sound proof curtains can help reduce external noises, or you might encourage your dog to sleep in a different room where there are fewer disturbances.

Not all sounds are disturbing: white noise can help block out external noise that might negatively impact on sleep, and may be worth trying; you could also try pink or brown noise to see which works best for your dog. White, pink and brown noise are produced by generating random noise across the sound spectrum. White noise is broadly spread across the sound spectrum, including low-frequency, mid-range and high-frequency sounds. Pink noise is white noise with reduced higher frequencies, while brown noise lowers the higher frequencies even more.

You can buy small portable machines, or download samples from YouTube; don't turn the volume up too loud – remember how acute a dog's hearing is. It may be best employed with some dogs as part of a pre-bedtime routine rather than during the night when it may cause your dog to sleep only lightly; again it is a case of trial and error to discover what is right for your dog.

Used as part of the pre-bedtime routine, playing music can also have a beneficial calming effect on both you and your dog, helping to relax you both and put you in the right state of mind. For preference, use recordings rather than the TV or radio, as it will give you more choice and greater control over what you listen to. Classical music has been shown in studies to have a soothing and relaxing influence; appropriately enough, Bach has proved to be a favourite. Reggae also appears to be favoured, but avoid any music which is too rousing, or has lots of drum rolls or clashing of cymbals.

Location

Locate your dog's bed in the room furthest away from the most likely sources of disturbances. Some dogs may be more settled and less likely to be aroused or become agitated by odd noises if they can sleep in your room if they don't already, so you might also give this consideration. Make sure it is in a draught-free space which can easily be darkened, as already mentioned.

Bed

Creating an inviting sleeping place is essential, and type of bed is as important as location; this aspect is covered in detail in Chapter 5.

Exercise

As well as being good for your dog's physical and mental health, appropriate levels of exercise and activity can contribute to better sleep habits. The key word here is 'appropriate': letting your dog overdo things or engaging him in the wrong sort of games can leave him sore and aching in his body, making it hard for him to sleep.

Lots of fast zooming around and over-exciting games can bump up adrenalin levels, which can remain in the system for many hours, so that rather than being ready to snooze come the evening, he is instead hyped-up and restless.

Low-intensity exercise will result in the lowering of epinephrine (adrenalin) levels, while low to moderate intensity exercise helps increase natural levels of serotonin.

This is the brain's 'feelgood' chemical, which produces feelings of calmness and contentment. Furthermore, it beneficially elevates dopamine levels: this is a neurotransmitter which amongst other things, is involved with the wake/sleep cycle. As well as avoiding fast, arousing games in the evening, if you can't send your dog out into the garden to toilet before bed, then the late night walk should therefore be a quiet stroll on the leash.

If possible, try to stick to quiet routes where you are less likely to meet noisy late night noisy revellers returning home from the pub or any wildlife. As sniffing can be a calming activity, allow him to also spend some time mooching around having a good sniff.

Toilet routine

Your dog isn't a young puppy or elderly, he has no health issues and doesn't wake you in the night because he's been disturbed, frightened or is hungry. But when you let him out in your garden for his last wee before bedtime, he does however, get over-excited. He rushes out excitedly, barking and scenting around all the bushes. It's dark, so you can't see him and when he comes back indoors you assume he has done his business. Wrong! If he is getting you up in the night needing to toilet, chances are he forgot to go earlier.

Just one encounter with a hedgehog, cat, or fox at this late hour can set up a pattern of overexcitement. His behaviour could also be disturbing the neighbours if he barks as he seeks out the imagined intruder. This over-arousal and forgetfulness can easily be curbed with some management and by teaching a cue word that he associates with toileting

The trick is to calm his excitement and manage the exit into the garden:

1. Have some treats ready and put him on his lead.

2. Ask him to sit and wait at the door into the garden. You can encourage and reinforce the sit and wait by feeding him a few treats rapidly one after the other. If he gets up before you release him, quietly ask for the sit again. Do not open the door until he is focused on you, and quiet.

3. Start to touch the handle and open the door slightly, but simultaneously reinforce the wait with your verbal cue. You can also feed him a few more treats and use your body to block him moving forward and squeezing through the crack of the now slightly open door. If you need to, you can work on this in the daytime, so he can be more successful at bedtime.

4. Once you can open the door all the way whilst he sits and waits, you can invite him to move with a release cue. This can be FREE, or RELEASE, but something that he will come to recognise as a clue that he can move from the position you have asked him to stay in. If he rushes out the door, as you release him scatter a few treats just outside the door for him to focus on.

5. Keep him on lead and walk around the garden with him. Once they have done a circuit of the garden on lead, some dogs will calm down enough to be let off lead to do their business, whilst others may need to be kept on lead the whole time. If he is still excited, bring him back inside and repeat the process from the beginning until he understands that you want calm behaviour.

6. After a while once he has mastered the routine, you may find you can just ask for the sit and wait at the door without putting his lead on. He now wanders out calmly once you release him.

• It can of course, be helpful to check your garden for wildlife before letting your dog outside. If you have an area he doesn't normally go into and which doesn't hold associations of meeting wildlife in (a front garden for example) take him there.

Teach a pee cue

Make sure your dog actually goes to the toilet when you let or take him out. If the garden is dark so you can't see what he is up to, set up some inexpensive solar-powered lighting or invest in a decent torch. Some dogs you may need to accompany, in all weathers (another reason they might not relieve themselves, as some hate the rain as much as us). Teaching your dog a 'pee command' is simple and worth doing, as it helps remind him why he is out there and can speed matters up considerably.

1. First, think of a word that you want to use as your pee cue. The most common words or phrases used are 'busy, busy' or 'hurry up', but you can choose whatever you like, as long as it is something you don't use often during everyday life, and which won't be embarrassing for you, or offensive to others, to use in public.

2. Whenever you take your dog out on a walk, or into the garden to toilet, wait until you see him actually peeing; only once he is in full flow say your chosen pee cue eg 'Busy, busy' or 'hurry up' and keep repeating it until he is done.

3. Once he has finished give him a huge amount of praise and a yummy treat (make sure you have remembered to take the treat out with you!) It is important that you give him the treat there and then, so he makes the connection between the action and reward.

4. Repeat this stage for a few days; you will find that you soon learn to recognise the visual cues he gives, just before he starts to toilet. Now is the time to introduce your pee cue, just before, or right as, he starts to go. Be sure that he is definitely about to start before you use the verbal cue though, or he won't make the connection between the word and the action. Do keep rewarding with treats and heaping on the praise as he finishes.

5. After a few more days, try giving the command when he looks as though he might be interested in going; give the pee cue and repeat it as he goes, praising lavishly and rewarding with a treat as he finishes, just as you have done previously. If you have misjudged matters, don't worry; simply repeat the earlier steps to establish more firmly the association between the pee cue and action and to give you more time to learn the little giveaway signs that he wants, or is about, to spend a penny.

6. Eventually, you will be able to say the word and it will encourage him to toilet; do continue to reward, with praise and/or a treat, even after he knows the command, to reinforce the behaviour. Some dogs are very quick to pick this cue up, while others can take a little longer to catch on; but all dogs can be taught it, regardless of age.

The good news is that most dogs calm down and toilet quickly once you have put these actions in place. Once his bladder is empty he should, unless ill, sleep through the night.

• Take your dog out to toilet before your relaxation time so as not to reawaken him just before bed. It can be useful to also carry out your night-time routine of locking doors, switching off electrical items and even performing your nightly ablutions, and then relaxing so you don't become more wakeful too.

Diet

It is fairly well documented that diet, in both humans and dogs can have a dramatic influence on behaviour as well as health. Precisely what constitutes a healthy and appropriate diet is a matter of much controversy, frequently provoking passionate and often heated debate: what all opinions do agree on however, is that products containing artificial preservatives, antioxidants and food colourings are generally best avoided. Artificial colourings in particular have been linked to hyperactivity.

So conversely, the diet and treats you feed him have the potential to enhance calmness. If you feed a commercially prepared kibble or tinned diet, choose one which is of good quality, but even so, read the labelling carefully. It can sometimes be confusing and ambiguous, so you may need to do a little extra research to find out more about the ingredients listed, and what they mean for your dog's health and welfare. Equally importantly, is what may have been left out, which could be vital for him to thrive.

Some diets can leave dogs hungry, especially growing adolescents, causing them to wake early. If you think this is the case, try feeding a small meal before bedtime or moving his main meal to later in the evening. You might also want to check whether his food has enough carbohydrates to keep him sated; if you have any questions about the optimal food for your dog, check with a pet nutritionist who can advise you. You'll find information about how to find one in the Resource Section.

Encouraging your dog to use his nose lowers the pulse rate and can be very calming just before bedtime, so food can also be utilised as a way of helping your dog decompress, just as listening to quiet music or reading a book might help you. His version of reading a book might be slowly searching for treats around a room, rummaging for small pieces of food in a snufflemat or having something to lick smeared on a Lickimat. A long lasting tasty natural chew will also relax him, allowing the release of soothing endorphins. Be careful about offering puzzle feeders, as some may cause frustration or excitement: choose things which help him to chill, rather than exciting him.

• As well as what you feed, frequency appears to have a bearing on sleep, and how well rested your dog is. Studies seem to indicate that dogs fed twice a day rather than once a day tend to go to sleep earlier at night. Although they also nap less frequently, they do so for longer periods.

Holidays

If you take your dog away on holiday, although he may find the excitement and novelty of being in a new environment great fun, he may also find aspects of it stressful and this can make it more difficult for him to sleep. Being tired from the day's activities doesn't necessarily mean he'll nod straight off (although many do); all those exciting experiences may mean he has a lot of adrenalin still coursing through his body, leaving him feeling wakeful and restless rather than relaxed and sleepy. Sleeping in a strange environment may also make him feel uneasy and wakeful as a result.

Make sure you take his own bedding from home as this will give him something familiar in a new place. If he can share your room, your presence close by may also assist in helping him feel safe and more likely to sleep – and if there are strange noises indoors or outside, it will be easier for you to reassure him if they make him anxious.

It can be beneficial if, as far as possible, you maintain your usual pre-bedtime routine.

Apart from having a soporific effect, it will be another comforting bit of familiarity to help him feel safe and ready to settle. You may also find it helpful to try one of the Adaptil or Pet Remedy calming products: you can find more information on this in Chapter 6.

As well as holidays away from home, there are also holidays at home to consider, which may involve changes to your dog's routine that he might find unsettling. Particularly at times like Christmas, there can be a lot going on to excite or worry him, including visitors arriving and departing, or guests staying over for the festivities, and who want to constantly pet or play games with him.

He may become very overstimulated, and although he will need his rest more than ever to cope, might find it difficult to achieve. It may be necessary for you to step in, using decompression activities and the other suggestions in this chapter to encourage him to switch off and take a nap if he is unable to do it himself.

Do make sure his bed is in a place where he isn't going to be constantly disturbed by a stream of people passing by or stepping over him – this can make him feel defensive as well as too anxious to sleep. A crate may be a good option if your dog is a denning type and will help ensure that he feels he has a secure space. If you need to relocate his bed somewhere for the duration of the stay of visitors, accustom him to it beforehand; or, as already mentioned, consider allowing him to sleep in your room, if you don't already.

You've probably already got house rules in place regarding the dog which your family are familiar with, but remember that visitors may not know them. Make sure they all know that his bed is his safe place and he's not to be disturbed when in there, and definitely not to be woken if he's sleeping.

Clock Changes

In those countries which use Daylight Saving Time, setting the clocks forward or backwards an hour can often leave you feeling a little jet-lagged and disoriented for a few days as your body adjusts to the new routine. While some dogs appear to take everything happening an hour earlier or later than usual in their stride, some find it confusing, challenging and stressful, and it can impact on their sleep routine.

Dogs can anticipate the time of routine daily events such as meals, walks, your arrival home from work and bedtime with uncanny accuracy.

This is because just like humans, they're influenced by circadian rhythms; these are physical, mental and behavioural changes which follow a 24-hour cycle. They are regulated by biological clocks present in nearly every tissue and organ of the body and kept in sync by a master clock in the brain, and affect wakefulness, alertness, and sleepiness, as well as energy levels and appetite. Although it's 'only' an hour, the sixty minute time change at the beginning and end of Daylight Saving Time can really throw things out of kilter and it can take a few days for the biological clock to reset.

When the clocks go backward, going to bed an hour later in the evening is less likely to be an issue for most dogs than waking up in the morning, when he will want to get up at the usual time – an hour earlier than the rest of the country. While you might enjoy the prospect of a lie-in, rising later may also mean an accident indoors if your dog isn't able to hold his bladder; an hour can seem a long time to wait if he's a real creature of habit.

When the clocks go forward, he may not be ready for sleep an hour early, although most seem to have less issue with rising earlier in the morning if it involves going out for a walk and having some breakfast.

You can help to reduce any anxiety and

minimise disruption to your dog's accustomed bedtime schedule caused by putting clocks backwards or forwards by gradually phasing in the change. If you can manage it, spread it out over a week, adjusting the time that the most predictable aspects of your dog's usual daily routine occur, such as toileting, walks, meals, playtime and bedtime by 10 minutes each day. You will also feel the benefit yourself as you gently ease into the new timetable rather than abruptly transitioning into it!

Bedtime Routine
Most dogs enjoy and benefit from having a regular routine, with continuity in terms of when certain activities such as walks, play, eating, and sleeping take place each day. Going to bed at roughly the same time each evening also helps to set the body clock, which can make it more likely that you will both sleep.

Including a pre-bedtime routine will also be beneficial, and can help you both to unwind at the end of the day so you're ready for sleep when you turn in for the night.

Relax: Spend at least half an hour in which to relax before bedtime yourself: dimming the lights will encourage the production of melatonin, helping to promote that sleepy feeling. Turn off the television, and put tablets and other screens away – their noise and light can often be as distracting and arousing for your dog as for you. Maybe play some quiet, soothing music or perhaps try some breathing exercises. Do whatever helps you to unwind, because as well as setting yourself up for a good night's sleep, very often your dog will copy you and be in a calmer, more settled state of mind, ready to doze off when it's bedtime.

And Breathe.....
If you find deep breathing exercises restful, you can even teach your dog to do them too. Breathing slowly and deeply triggers the parasympathetic nervous system (the rest and digest part of the nervous system) promoting relaxation and helping to quiet the mind, as well as countless other benefits. Teaching dogs to regulate their oxygen intake to promote relaxation is simpler than you think; spending a few minutes practicing this each night can become a part of your pre-bedtime routine.

1. Take a pot of small soft treats and sit on the floor in a quiet room with your dog. Hold a treat in your fist up by your nose – but only if your dog is polite and won't jump up at your face. Start to take deep breaths and exhale slowly and audibly. If you sit slightly to the side, you can watch your dog's ribcage. When you see an intake of breath, feed a treat.

2. If you need to encourage a breath, let your dog sniff the treat held in your closed fist, holding it halfway between your face and his, and when you see a flare of the nostrils, immediately open your fist and feed. Keep repeating this routine of breathe – feed – breathe – feed, but try to start targeting the deeper inhalations.

3. Eventually over multiple sessions you will be able to add a cue word like 'chill' so he will take a deep breath on cue, or your own inbreath can become the cue. This is useful for hyperactive dogs as it promotes rest. It focuses the mind and stills the nerves whilst calming the body.

Tellington TTouch® for restfulness

Applying some of the Tellington TTouch body work and other tools can also form part of the solution to aiding a peaceful night's sleep. Spending some time at any point in the day or evening giving your dog a nice TTouch (pronounced Tee-Touch) body work session can be calming and soothing, and is certainly worth incorporating into a pre-bedtime routine. The benefits can be mutual too; because it can be as enjoyable and relaxing for you to give as for your dog to receive, it can be the perfect way of appreciating each other's company and preparing for a restful night.

Anyone can learn to do the TTouch body work; no special knowledge of anatomy is needed, and most dogs love it. There are many different 'TTouches', the name used for the specialised ways of moving the skin around. A few simple TTouch body work exercises are included here for you to try; if you and your dog enjoy them and you would like to learn more, we recommend that you buy a copy of *Getting in TTouch with your Dog* by the method's founder, Linda Tellington Jones. You might also like to attend workshops or demonstrations, or work one-to-one with a TTouch practitioner. You can also watch the TTouches being demonstrated online by visiting You Tube and searching for Tellington TTouch for dogs – you will find plenty of video clips.

Getting started

Be sure not to lean over your dog while doing the TTouches, as this might intimidate or frighten him. It is safer for you and more comfortable for your dog if you position yourself to the side of, and just behind his head, so you are both facing in the same direction. This will enable you to see him and to monitor his responses clearly but without staring directly at him which he may find confrontational. It also makes it easy for him to move away if he wishes, without having to go through you in order to do so.

The special TTouches involve gently moving the skin in various ways. They are calming and reassuring, helping your dog to relax by flipping him from the sympathetic (flight and fight side of the nervous system) into the parasympathetic nervous system (rest and digest side of the nervous system), releasing tension and lowering his stress levels. It takes only a short time to learn how to produce a beneficial effect, although the more you practise, the better you will become at it, and the more your dog will look forward to, and enjoy, your special quality-time together. It will also help him to feel sleepy and ready to settle down.

Spend around twenty minutes on each session, although do not feel you have to keep one eye fixed on the clock; this is just a guideline. Younger dogs may prefer a shorter session, and older dogs may enjoy a slightly longer one, but allow your dog to be your guide in this respect. Signs that he may need a break include him looking unsettled, moving away from you, becoming distracted, and fidgeting. Stop for a while and allow your dog to reposition himself. If he readily settles down for some more work, continue, but if he responds again in a similar way, then end the session.

Sometimes a dog may appear not to enjoy the TTouches, and if this is the case, stop, but do ask your vet to check him over in case there is a health issue. If he gets the all-clear, seek the assistance of a qualified Tellington TTouch Practitioner to help you in introducing the work.

- **If your dog wishes to move away** while you are doing the TTouches, allow him to do so.

- **Let him choose his position:** do not insist that he stands if he feels more comfortable sitting or lying down. In fact lying on his bed, or next to you, will encourage him to settle for the evening.

- **Practise doing each of the TTouches on your own arms** or on a partner or friend's arms or back before trying them on your pet. This will help you to appreciate just how light and subtle you can be. Another human can also give you feedback on how it feels and help you to improve.

- **Concentrating on what you are doing** can sometimes make you stiff and tense, which will make the TTouches feel unpleasant to the recipient. Try to relax and keep your breathing deep and regular. Allowing your dog to hear you breathe deeply and *slowly* will also encourage him to match his rate of breathing to yours, aiding calmness and encouraging relaxation.

- **Just the weight of your hand is enough to move the skin** while performing each of the TTouches. At no time should you press into the body; you are only working with the skin.

- **Make each of your TTouches as slow as possible.** Two to three seconds is a good guide for each repetition of one of the movements.

- **Should your dog show concern** about you touching certain parts of his body, return to a place where he is less anxious, and when he relaxes try gradually approaching the difficult area again. Other signs such as stiffness, or tautness or changes in temperature of the skin, or changes in the hair colour, direction and texture of the coat, may indicate the presence of a physical problem; ask your vet to investigate further.

Does he like it?

If you are a little unsure about reading your dog's body language and want to check that he really is comfortable with the body work rather than just tolerating it, simply do one or two repetitions of the TTouch you are performing and stop.

Take your hands off your dog and move back a little from him. If he re-engages with you by looking in your direction, or moving closer, by nudging your arm or maybe softly whining, then continue doing a few more TTouches.

Continue to check-in often with him, by regularly stopping and asking for permission to continue. If he moves away when you stop, let him. He may need a drink, or to 'think' about how the work feels. Often he will return and re-engage with you and you can continue, but if not, don't force it. Some animals really do need the work drip fed in micro-sessions, so be led by your dog and give him the choice. He may even very well take himself off for a sleep whilst the work processes through the cells of his body.

Ear TTouch

Ear work can have a wonderfully calming, comforting and soothing effect, helping to lower stress levels, and breath and heart rate when done slowly. Human babies often play with their ears at bedtime. It can also help adults to drift off if done slowly; try it to experience how it feels.

The majority of dogs enjoy Ear TTouches, and most owners naturally stroke their dog's ears anyway. Note that for the purposes of TTouch only one ear is stroked at a time, swapping often between the two.

1.

Position yourself so that both you and your dog are facing in the same direction. Lightly place one hand on his body. Use the back of your other hand to stroke softly along the outside of one ear.

2.

If your dog is happy about this, cup your hand around the ear and stroke from the base to the tip. Try to mould as much of your hand as possible around his ear for maximum contact. Follow the natural direction of the ear; if your dog has upright ears work in an upwards direction: if they flop downwards, work in a horizontal outwards and downwards direction.

3.

Next, take the ear between the thumb and curved forefingers of one hand so that you only have one layer of ear flap between fingers and thumb. Slide them along the length of the ear, working from the base right out to the end or tip. Move your hand slightly each time you begin a new stroke so that you cover every part of the ear. Be gentle and work slowly to help calm and relax. At the tip of the ear is an acupressure 'shock' point: make a small circle there with the tip of your forefinger to stimulate it, and then slide your fingers off. This is beneficial for dogs that are habitually nervous or have trouble settling down to sleep.

4.

If your dog is holding his ears in a furled, pinned or high ear carriage, very gently unfurl or lower them as you slide along each ear, bringing it into a more natural, relaxed position. Posture can directly affect behaviour, so if the ears are relaxed the rest of the body will tend to follow suit.

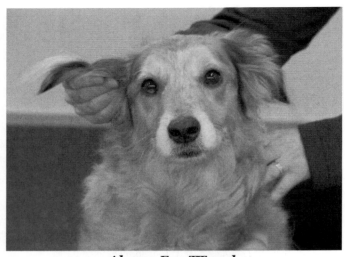

Above: Ear TTouch
(Image©Toni Shelbourne)

5.

If your dog appears to dislike ear work and has floppy ears, try moulding your hand over one and gently holding it against his head. Very slowly and gently move your whole hand in a circular movement, so that his head supports his ear. Make the circle small so that it is a subtle movement; he may prefer it being circled in an anti-clockwise direction to a clockwise one. If he still finds this challenging, try wearing a sheepskin mitten or glove to diffuse the sensation even further. You may find that this will help to reduce any concerns he has and to become more tolerant about ear work. If he continues to show concern, do ask your vet to check his ears, mouth and neck, as there may be an underlying physical reason for his unease.

• Be careful if your dog has ongoing ear problems, as he may be defensive of you touching them. If so, skip this TTouch and move on to the next.

Zebra TTouch

This is a good TTouch to use with busy dogs who are overly sensitive about contact, and who may dislike being petted.

It's great for gaining the attention of a nervous and excitable dog, and can help him settle quickly ready for bed.

1.

Position yourself to one side of your dog – he can be sitting, standing or lying down. Start with your fingers and thumb relaxed and gently curved. (*See Picture A*)

Resting your hand on the top of his shoulder, slide your hand downwards over the opposite side of his body from where you are positioned, allowing your thumb and fingers to spread apart as it moves down over the shoulder blade, towards the top of your dog's foreleg (*see Picture B*)

2.

As your hand comes back up towards the spine, allow the fingers to loosely close together again.

Your fingers should be in contact with the skin; keep the pressure light, but firm enough that you don't tickle – think of your fingers gliding over the skin, not pressing into it. (*see Picture C*).

With a longer coated dog you may find your fingers sink into his coat, so take care if you encounter a tangle.

3.

Change the angle of your hand slightly each time you complete an upwards or downwards movement so that your hand travels along the length of your dog's body from shoulder to hindquarters in a zigzag pattern. (*see Picture D*).

When you've finished, switch sides and repeat, unless he is lying flat on one side, in which case just work on the area you can reach.

4.

If your dog is wary of you leaning over him, or you can't reach the opposite side of his body from you, try doing the same movement with the back of your hand on the side of the body closest to you.

Above: Zebra TTouch picture A
(©Toni Shelbourne)

Above: Zebra TTouch picture B
(Image©Toni Shelbourne)

Above: Zebra TTouch picture C
(Image©Toni Shelbourne)

Above: Zebra TTouch picture D
(Image©Toni Shelbourne)

Abalone TTouch

This TTouch can be very calming, warming and comforting so it's perfect for helping a dog to relax and settle for the night.

As well as producing a sense of comfort and sleepiness, it is great for wellbeing and helping to relieve any feelings of stiffness so may be particularly beneficial for an elderly dog, or a younger one who may have overdone things.

Generally it is easiest to start on your dog's shoulder area and work out from there, returning to this region if need be.

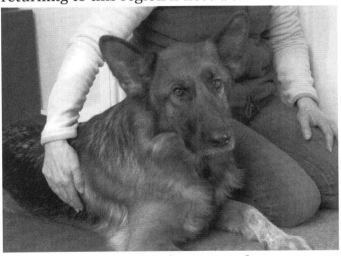

Above: Abalone TTouch
(Image©Toni Shelbourne)

1.

Position yourself to the side and slightly behind your dog. Softly place the whole of your hand on the opposite side of your dog's body, moulding the fingers, thumb and palm to the contours of the shoulder. The thumb should be a little apart from the fingers in a narrow V shape, to help steady your hand. Your wrist should be straight and relaxed at all times to enable the hand to rotate as you perform the movement. You can place your other hand, as a balance, on the opposite side of the body your original hand is placed, if your dog is comfortable with two hands in contact. The second hand just supports but doesn't do any of the TTouches, generally these should only be performed with one hand.

2.

Using the whole of the hand, gently move your dog's skin in a clockwise circle about 1 cm in diameter. Maintain the same speed for the whole movement. It helps if you imagine that your hand is travelling around a clock face: start each circle where the six would be and move in a clockwise direction all the way around the dial – but when you return to the six position again, keep on going to nine o'clock on the clock face so that you have completed one full circle plus a quarter of another one. (*see Circular TTouch Picture E*) Try to make your circles as slow as possible.

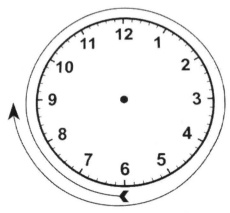

Above: Circular TTouch picture E

3.

Keep your wrist and hand relaxed, and maintain a light but consistent pressure and speed. Do not press into your dog's skin – use no more than just the weight of your hand. After completing each TTouch, stop, and keeping your hand in contact with your dog, pause for a slow breath and then slide your hand lightly across the coat to a new spot about a hands' width away and begin another circle.

4.

Remember to start each circle at the 'six' point, with six being the point nearest to the ground or your dog's undercarriage. Ensure that the skin feels as though you are lightly lifting not dragging it as you start each circle - experiment on your own arm to check.

5.

Remember that you should be moving the skin with your hand, rather than allowing your hand to glide over the surface. If your dog is long coated, you may find it more effective to lightly reposition your fingers into the coat slightly so you can more easily feel his skin.

6.

When working over bony areas, or places where he is concerned about being touched, make your contact with your dog's body much lighter, so you are hardly touching him at all while still moving the skin under your hand. If the skin feels tight, do not try and force it to move, but try making just a quarter circle, then a half, building up to a full circle and a quarter as the skin becomes more malleable under your hand. Continue to use the lightest of pressures and to be very slow in your movement.

7.

If your dog doesn't like 'connected' TTouches, (i.e. when you link each TTouch by sliding your fingers across the skin from the circle you have just completed to the place where you are going to start the next one, maintaining a constant light contact), try lifting your hand after each circle instead and gently placing it somewhere else on his body. Experiment to see which works best for your dog, and bear in mind that preferences may change from day to day or even hour to hour. Sometimes working randomly over your dog's body can grab the attention of the nervous system better than 'connected' TTouches.

8.

If your dog still appears reluctant about allowing you to work on certain areas of his body, move back to a place where he enjoys the feel of the TTouch and dip in and out of the areas of concern as described previously. You could also do the same movement with the back of your hand or with little contact with the back of the fingers. We call this TTouch the Llama; it feels much less invasive than the front of the hand and can therefore be more acceptable to some dogs.

9.

Lots of dogs really enjoy this TTouch on their chest, shoulders and neck. Combined with the Ear TTouch and the Coiled Python it can be very settling.

Coiled Python

The Coiled Python is a combination TTouch where a lift of the skin is incorporated with a circular TTouch such as the Abalone mentioned above.

The circular part of the TTouch heightens the dog's focus and the lift helps him to relax and brings attention to what you are doing. It helps to relax tense areas of skin and muscle, which is particularly relevant for hyperactive dogs who find it difficult to settle.

This TTouch can be done with any part of the front of the hand, so the pads, or half the length of the fingers, or the whole hand in the abalone configuration which can be very relaxing.

1.

With the whole hand moulded to an area of your dog's body, move the skin in a circle and a quarter, just as you do with the Abalone TTouch (if you have not yet read about or practised the Abalone yet, return to this section first to learn how to perform a circular TTouch). However, when you reach the nine o'clock position, carry the tissue a little further around the clock face, without pausing, to twelve o'clock, but being careful not to pull the skin.

2.

Once at twelve o'clock pause for a moment before slowly allowing the tissue back around the half circle from twelve o'clock to six o'clock, but this time moving in an anti-clockwise direction from twelve o'clock through nine o'clock and finishing at six o'clock. You will feel the skin wanting to resettle, your job is to support it back down and not drop it into place. If you simply let go of the skin while it is at the twelve o'clock position, it will feel like a sudden lurch to your dog as the skin falls back into place; a most unpleasant sensation.

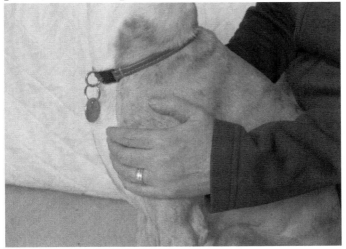

Above: Coiled Python TTouch
(Image©Toni Shelbourne)

3.

The slower you can carry and support the tissue back around the half circle from twelve o'clock to the six o'clock position, the more benefit your dog will feel and you should notice a softening of the tension in the area you are working.

4.

Once you have completed the movement, leave your hand in place, pausing for a few seconds before moving to a new area and repeating.

The Half Wrap

Body wraps can be used in a variety of different configurations to help in resolving a wide number of issues; in this case it can help calm your dog ready for sleep or prepare him for wearing a warm fleece coat overnight which might aid slumber if he feels the cold.

Provided you introduce it properly, most dogs enjoy wearing a wrap, but even if you think your pet looks a bit comical in it, don't laugh at him - dogs can be just as sensitive as people about being ridiculed.

1.

Approach your dog calmly with the wrap, and with it bundled up in your hand, let him sniff at, and take a good look at it. Do not rush this stage.

Stroke it gently against his sides and chest. You can even use it to do some circular TTouches on his shoulders and chest. If he is anxious about approaching it, place the wrap on the floor and put treats on top of it for him to eat.

2.

Once your dog is quite happy around the wrap, unroll and pass the centre of the bandage around the front of his chest. Bring the ends up across the shoulders, up over his back and cross them over just above his shoulder blades.

Above: TTouch Half Wrap
(Image©Toni Shelbourne)

3.

Take both loose ends down the sides of his ribcage, behind the front legs. Cross them beneath his rib cage and bring them back up again over the top of his back.

As you do this, keep the wrap close to his body and unravel it a little at a time from your hands so it doesn't flap around. Be careful not to inadvertently pull the ends too much at this stage, as some dogs may find this difficult to cope with. Try to be slow and smooth in your movements.

4.

Tie the ends in a bow or quick release knot so it can be quickly undone again if necessary. Make sure that the fastening lies off to one side of the spine, not directly on top of it. Alternatively, sew some Velcro to the bandage ends to secure it.

The wrap should be applied just firmly enough to keep it in place and enable it to maintain contact with the body – about the same sort of pressure as an elasticated tracksuit waistband.

Check in various places to see if you can easily slide your hand beneath it. If it is too tight in one area and too loose in another, readjust it until the tension is the same throughout.

Remember that its purpose is to provide feelings of security and sensory input, not to support, and it certainly shouldn't restrict movement or cause discomfort.

5.

Encourage your dog to move while wearing the wrap: if he freezes, use gentle coaxing, offer a really tasty treat or invite a gentle game with a favourite toy to overcome his reluctance. If he rubs or grabs at it, try to distract him. If after a few minutes he is still worrying at it or not moving, remove it and try again on another day.

Before applying the wrap again, do more TTouches on him by way of preparation for wearing it.

6.

Even if your dog seems comfortable the first time he wears a wrap, remove it after a few minutes, and over the next few sessions gradually increase the duration it is worn for. Do not rush this process or be tempted to put it on before he is comfortable settling down with it on.

Never leave your dog alone while he is wearing a wrap or overnight in case he gets caught up or has had enough of it. Keep a close eye on him in case you need to make adjustments for comfort or safety, or if he wants it taken off. On very rare occasions some dogs appear to not tolerate body wraps at all. This may be down to an underlying health or pain issue so do consult your vet.

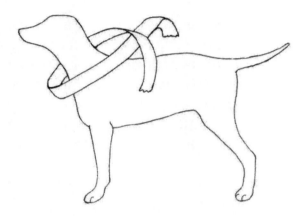

TTOUCH HALF WRAP

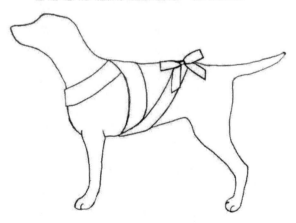

Above: Tying a TTouch Half Wrap

You can find out more about using body wraps in 'All Wrapped Up For Pets: Improving function, performance and behaviour with Tellington TTouch Body Wraps' by Robyn Hood (see Further Reading).

4
PUPPIES

For many years the advice given to new puppy parents was that it was fine for their 8-week-old charge to be left on his own in a separate room to sleep at night.

If he vocalised, guardians should not go down to him, but let the puppy cry it out. Sadly, this advice is still often heard, with many people reporting that they adopt it - thankfully some give up and spend the night with their puppy. This method is not only outdated, but can be actively harmful to a young dog's health, setting him up for a lifetime of anxiety about being alone.

Above: Sleep is essential for all dogs, and especially so for puppies.
(Image©Toni Shelbourne)

Social sleepers

In nature, free-roaming mothers continue to have a relationship with their young long past the eight weeks of age when your puppy will have been deemed ready to leave for his new home. Dogs are social sleepers. If you observe a litter of puppies, you will notice that they sleep in close contact with their siblings and mother, and will become distressed if separated. At this tender age they are unable to fully regulate their body temperature and still need the emotional support of each other and their mother. Wild dogs and feral puppies tend to stay together and will continue to sleep in a pile on top of one another for at least five months, not becoming independent sleepers until adolescence.

Compare this to the situation of a mere two month old pup: he has just been removed from everything and everyone he knows, experiencing numerous novel and frightening experiences in the process – and is then expected to settle at night all on his own in a strange and possibly frightening new environment. It is neither reasonable nor compassionate: your puppy may never have been exposed to isolation either in wake or sleep. He won't know you, the environment, or what is expected of him: he may feel cold, frightened and emotionally overwhelmed. He has already had so much to process on this first day with you, and sleep is the best way of helping him make sense of this new world - so a negative experience on the first and subsequent nights is counterproductive, and not conducive to bonding or future positive experiences of being alone.

Puppies are known to have better quality and duration of sleep when they have company. This allows the important functions of sleep such as boosting the immune system, as well as emotional processing, and memory consolidation to be optimised.

Studies of human young who are left to cry demonstrate that it has the reverse effect of teaching independence. Repeatedly allowing an infant to become distressed creates issues such as insecure attachments and demanding, clingy behaviour: with a growing body of evidence that brain structure and function in all mammals is similar, it's not surprising that similar behaviours are seen in dogs, too, with a pattern of separation anxiety often emerging.

First nights and months
Whether you ultimately want your puppy to sleep in a different room or not, it is vital that

his first night and indeed his first few months is spent with a human nearby in the same room. This has lots of advantages as you can tell if he needs toileting (which will decrease the time it takes you to toilet train him) or if he is ill, frightened, or cold.

Ideally, set up an area by your bed so that if your puppy is restless, you are more likely to hear him, and it is easier to reach down to comfort him. A small area is best as you don't necessarily want him to wander around and toilet as you sleep. You can use a puppy pen, crate, or large box: it should have a cosy, soft bed, and if it's winter, a safe source of warmth. If you have an item that smells of his mother – or failing that, of you - pop it in with your puppy to snuggle up to, or if you are willing, sleep with your puppy touching you.

If you are a light sleeper and hear him starting to move around during the night, it will most likely be because he needs to toilet. Take him out, encourage him to toilet, then pop him straight back in his sleeping area. Don't overly fuss or stimulate him and he should drop right back off to sleep again. Note the time so you can keep a record to help you set him up for success.

If you are a heavy sleeper, set an alarm to

wake you at an appropriate time to take your puppy out to toilet. Each dog will be different, but puppies tend to toilet less at night as they are eating and drinking less. Start by maybe waking and popping him outside twice during the night, reducing to once when you can see he can hold himself. Keep a diary of when he generally goes and how long he can hold himself and that will give you a good idea of how often you need to take him out. If he has an accident, note the time and take him out sooner the next night.

Bedtime routine
Dim the lights in the evening and if he's awake try some soothing slow, long strokes. Before bed, a meal and an opportunity to toilet will encourage him to sleep. For safety, remove his collar at night, but if he needs to toilet, pop it on and attach his lead so you are close by and can see when he has relieved himself. Make sure you don't over stimulate him with play or rough handling.

Once in his sleeping area, he may need physical contact for a short time before dropping off so don't rush to remove yourself until you can see he is settled. If he's an anxious puppy, using Adaptil (see Chapter 6) might help; if using a plug-in diffuser make sure he can't get at it overnight, or indeed at any other electrical items or cables.

Once he's sleeping through the night, can hold his toilet until morning and happily settles to sleep on his own during the day with you absent, you can start to wean him from the bedroom if you want him eventually to sleep elsewhere. Do this slowly, beginning by moving his sleeping area further away from you, in tiny increments - a few centimetres at a time – over a period of several weeks. When his bed reaches the doorway, you may find setting up a baby gate useful so he can still see you from outside the bedroom: set up a second baby gate if he is sleeping on the landing at the top of a staircase, so there is no risk of him falling down them.

Sleeping with other adult dogs

Existing adult dogs will need time to adjust to the newcomer. It is normal for them to take several months to fully accept a puppy. You will need to set up separate areas initially, so your adult dog has his own space where he is not constantly having to put up with the attentions of a rambunctious puppy. Expecting him to sleep with and babysit the youngster over the first few months is unrealistic and potentially dangerous for the puppy if your adult dog is having trouble adjusting and disciplines the puppy inappropriately.

An adult dog who sleeps downstairs won't mind the puppy being in your bedroom at first. Once you know your puppy and dog have bonded, are comfortable in each other's company, and you have house trained your puppy, that is a better time to introduce sleeping together at night.

It's a gradual process: you may notice they begin to spend time close to each other when sleeping during the day, and that your puppy is now confident to take himself off to sleep without you nearby. You will also have been able to practice and observe his behaviour when left for short periods, either with you in another room or out of the house, whilst you watch on a camera.

Troubleshooting poor puppy sleep

Dogs are crepuscular ie they are most active at dawn and dusk, and you may have noticed your young dog gets a spurt of activity as the sun goes down. It is also the reason why many adolescence dogs wake early. It takes time for them to adjust to our rhythms, so be patient when your young dog wakes you at 5am ready to start his day. You can add on a few minutes at a time before you get up to encourage him to lie-in.

Chapters 2 and 3 explain why your dog may be sleeping poorly or waking at night, and offer suggestions as ways in which you can remedy them, but a few other things specific to puppies and adolescents, should also be considered:

• Hunger: like human children, growing dogs need adequate and frequent intake of nutrition. We tend to feed dogs when it suits us, but it doesn't always align with their needs. Make sure you spread his meals out and compensate for changing intake needs as he rapidly grows in his first few months. As already mentioned, a small meal last thing at night might help sleep.

• However, try not to make the mistake of feeding your adolescent dog or puppy really early in the morning, as if he is hungry or expecting a meal, he's more likely to wake you early! Again, a meal last thing at night and slowly extending the time you get up in the morning can help.

• If your puppy hasn't had enough mental stimulation or exercise during the day, he may be less likely to want to settle down at night.

• Lack of company: add up the time you are present with your dog during a 24-hour period. You may be surprised at how little quality time you actually spend with him!

• Illness, growing pains, upset digestion, feeling the effects of vaccinations etc. will ultimately impact on the quality of sleep.

Sleep is one of the foundation stones of life; it is essential for all animals, but especially important for young ones. How you deal with your puppy's sleeping pattern now could ultimately affect him for life, whether in a good or negative way, so it's well worth considering what he needs to sleep well, securely, and safely.

5
BEDS

Beds come in all shapes, sizes, colours and fabrics, and at prices to suit all pockets, from bargain basement to high-end. But just as you may have personal preferences about bed mattresses, so do dogs; some like to curl, others to sprawl, or tunnel or to create a nest in a pile of blankets. These preferences may vary throughout the day and the season as well as with age as they grow older and less mobile – or at any time in life if there are health issues. Observing him will help you make the right bed choices on his behalf.

The right bed
Access: The first consideration is that the bed must be easy for your dog to get into and out of; it sounds an obvious point, but is often overlooked. Really deep, soft beds or beanbags may look appealing to you – they can be very comfy to lie in and mould beautifully to the body, but if they move around a lot beneath him can be very difficult to rise from, especially if he is ageing or has mobility issues.

Raised sides can also create access issues if

your dog has trouble stepping over them: with this sort of bed, look for a low edge on one side that will allow him to step in easily.

Shape and size: Equally essential is shape and size of bed; posture can have a huge effect on behaviour, and a bed which restricts movement or enforces a sleeping posture can cause issues and potentially impact on quality of sleep. It's important that the bed allows your dog to adopt a variety of different positions. Although he may want to curl up sometimes, being able to stretch out full length as well is important for REM sleep.

Basic mattress shapes are generally easy for dogs to get on and off, and allow your dog to adopt any sleeping position he likes, but many do seem to like having sides to snuggle up against, and they do help in keeping floor-level draughts out. Rigid plastic shell type beds with curved sides can however force them to adopt a curled position, leading to tension within the body unless they are big enough – most owners underestimate the size their dog really needs. Think of how stiff you feel the next day after sleeping on a sofa that is too small! Beds with soft sides and cushioned bases can give more choice in position than rigid shells, but even so, make sure it is large enough: go a size bigger than you think you'll need so as to allow for a variety of sleeping positions, including lying flat out.

Above: The right bed can make all the difference to quality of sleep
(Image©Cressida Staddon)

Height: Some dogs prefer to sleep on a bed which is elevated, and it also helps to keep them out of any draughts. Raised beds may however, be a challenge for less mobile dogs to get onto, and depending on design, may have a risk of them rolling off the side while asleep. A ramp may solve the problem of access, but should be wide and stable enough to be safe and ensure there is no danger of mis-stepping off the side.

Support: Obviously a bed must be

comfortable or it won't be used. Like us, dogs are individuals and some like a firmer bed while others prefer a softer one. It should however, provide support and cushioning for joints – particularly for older dogs who may be more prone to callouses on hocks and elbows - but without causing strain or difficulty in rising from and getting out of it. Memory foam is often a popular choice for orthopaedic beds – the thicker the foam, generally the better the support.

Warmth: Some dogs do feel the cold at night; as well as very young and senior dogs, those with fine single coats may also appreciate a cosy bed. Raised sides will help keep out draughts, or providing sleeping bag and 'cave' type beds can be a solution – providing they can work out how to tunnel into them; some may need assistance initially, but some never seem to grasp the technique! A duvet can be another solution and many dogs enjoy burrowing beneath them and creating their own warm nest.

In summer, some beds may be too warm and a cooler surface preferred; providing an additional bed with a cooler fabric surface or a cool mat will offer choice.

Fabric: Fabrics must be sturdy enough to

withstand wear and tear – especially if your dog is one of those who likes to circle and maybe dig a bit in his bed before he settles to sleep. Tough fabrics may be required with puppies who may be exploring and testing everything with their teeth; and if your dog has mobility issues, avoid fabrics which his claws might snag and catch in.

Washability is also important; choose beds with removable covers for preference as these will be easy to launder and quick to dry. Some beds come with an additional inner waterproof cover, but if not adding one can be a good idea with dogs not yet housetrained or those who are incontinent. Alternatively you can add puppy pads or human incontinence pads (which are often cheaper and larger), although these may move around, or buy a reusable and more eco-friendly and stable special fabric mattress which will wick moisture away from a leaky dog.

Pillows: Like us, many dogs like to have a pillow - some will even seek out or carry a favourite cushion around on which to rest their heads. If you notice that your dog enjoys resting with his head higher than his body, try to provide a means for him to do so. Some bed designs incorporate a raised pillow area, but avoid any where such features are permanently fixed, as it is important that your dog has choice in his resting and sleeping position.

Above: Some dogs like to have a pillow to rest their head on
(Image©Charlotte Bull)

Crates

For dogs who like denning, a crate can be the

perfect place in which to snooze; place some bedding inside, throw a blanket over the top and you have an instant cosy cave. It can also be a comforting retreat during scary events such as thunder and fireworks, or enable him to find seclusion if you have visitors.

Even if a crate is not your dog's favoured place to rest, it is nevertheless worthwhile spending some time doing crate training, as there may be occasions when it is necessary for your dog to spend some time in one – if he is recovering from an operation or injury for example, and needs to be contained in order to minimise movement. It can also be a useful way of containing him in the car when travelling, and should he ever need to be admitted as a patient at the vet's, he'll be accustomed to being confined in an enclosed space and less likely to be anxious about it.

Crates come in all shapes and sizes including square, rectangular and tubular, and made of a variety of materials including steel mesh, fabric and plastic. Whatever type of crate you select, it must be large enough to allow your dog to stand up, lie down and comfortably turn around in when the bedding is in place. It should also be big enough that it doesn't enforce a sleeping position, but allows your dog to adopt whatever posture he prefers.

Spend some time introducing the crate to your dog. Set it up in a room where your dog will feel relaxed and confident. Place some comfy bedding inside, and pop toys and treats in for him to discover. This will encourage him to use it, and make it an inviting haven with pleasant associations where he will voluntarily choose to spend time relaxing. Never try and manhandle him inside, no matter how gentle you are about it!

You can however, introduce a verbal cue 'Crate!' or similar whenever you spot him going into it, so that you can ask him to go in on those occasions when you want him to. Tossing a treat in there for him to eat will enable you to repeat and establish this process more quickly. Leave the door open at all times initially, so he can come and go as he wishes; only when he is happy to spend time in there voluntarily should you shut the door. This should be for just a minute or two at first; provide a long-lasting treat such as a tightly stuffed Kong, or choose a time of day when he normally enjoys a nap so he is less likely to be concerned about it. Stay close by so you can let him out if he starts showing any signs of distress. Don't let him get to the stage where he is crying, barking or pawing at the bars. If he isn't comfortable yet, go back a stage in training.

Gradually you can increase the length of time you leave the door shut; how quickly you progress depends on how quickly he takes to the crate. While most dogs enjoy 'denning' especially if the crate is covered, as it provides them with a private, quiet space where they can feel safe, do not abuse this. Never leave your dog crated for more than two hours, and never unattended during the introductory process. In general daily use as a 'bedroom', leave the door open at all times so your dog can freely enter and exit as he wishes. As a polyphasic sleeper he may wake and want to move around, and depending on the time of year may also decide to move to a cooler or warmer spot for his next phase of sleep.

Extra warmth
You may be snuggled up all toasty and warm under your duvet while the heating is switched off at night, but your dog may be feeling chilly, which will make it hard for him to sleep and may make him restless or even to become vocal. It is not just a winter issue either; during the summer months, there can sometimes be a big temperature drop at night.

Cosy fleece PJs for dogs can offer a solution, but they aren't suitable for all canines. Some will build up static, so your dog receives little shocks when he moves: others will manage to become entangled in them, no matter the design, with legs tightly wedged through neck holes, or back legs trapped so they can't rise. If he becomes too warm, it is also difficult for him to cool down. If your dog sleeps in your room at night, and you are a light enough sleeper that you will rouse and be aware if he gets into difficulties, they may be a happy option for both of you, but otherwise be aware of the need for safety.

Other options include self-warming thermal bedding to line his bed, with plenty of warm blankets or old duvets to burrow under and snuggle into; some dogs appear however, to lack the skills to do so and will cry until a blanket which has fallen off is replaced for them! For some dogs, a sleeping bag or cave type bed solves the problem of slipping blankets.

Hot water bottles and microwaveable heated pads are generally best avoided because of the dangers if they burst or are chewed; similarly electric blankets.

Location, location, location
The location of your dog's bed can be as important to getting quality sleep as its type. It needs to be situated somewhere he can relax completely and sleep deeply, confident that he

won't be disturbed. Especially if you have a busy household, a safe and quiet place to retreat to when he wants peace and quiet can be essential for emotional and psychological health.

The ideal place should be draft free; check by lying down on the floor yourself; you may be surprised at the difference in temperature and amount of air movement. It should also be located away from areas where people or other pets are constantly passing. This can be particularly important with elderly dogs, whose lack of mobility may make them feel vulnerable, increasing the likelihood of them acting defensively at anyone approaching too closely. Anxious rescue dogs also need and will appreciate a secure place in which to curl up throughout the day.

Individual preferences vary so should also be taken into account. Some dogs like to be in a sheltered place such as a covered crate; some fitted kitchens are even designed with special 'dog nooks' or you could create something similar in understairs areas. Others prefer to have space above and around them or even to be up high. Observe your dog, and if you notice that he has a favoured sleeping spot, move his bed to there.

Better still, if you have the space available,

providing multiple beds in different places around the house is not as mad as it might sound, but instead provides your dog with choice, both in bed type and where he wants to sleep.

A study conducted in 2020 revealed that 30% of puppies and 44% of adult dogs will choose more than one place to snooze when given the option. You may find that he moves around them throughout the day; note his choices as it may indicate physical issues that warrant veterinary investigation, or emotional mindset.

If the room your dog sleeps in at night has a window or glass panelled door which looks out onto a patio or garden area, wildlife outside or external security lighting going off and on may wake him. A busy street may be equally disruptive, with passing people and traffic causing disturbance.

Hanging blackout or acoustic curtains may solve the problem, but if not, you may need to encourage your dog to sleep in a different room.

Bushes, tree branches and other foliage scraping against windows may also cause him to become anxious, but can be easily dealt with by a pair of garden secateurs or branch loppers.

Sharing your bed

"It's a two dog night" and "Throw another dog

Above: Sharing your bed can have pros and cons

(Image©Lizi Arnold)

on the bed" aren't just jokey ways of saying the weather is cold: rich man or poor man,

111

commoner or royal, humans and dogs have been bedfellows for centuries.

It's not just a question of human preferences: a study conducted in 2020 revealed that when given the choice, the majority of dogs – 86% – preferred to sleep close by their guardians at night.

In various polls which have been conducted in recent years, nearly 50% of dog guardians have admitted to allowing their canine companions to share their beds.

If you have no health concerns such as allergies, asthma or respiratory issues and both you and your dog are happy to share your sleeping place, that's fine.

You may need to change the bedding more frequently to keep on top of any doggy smell and the inevitable shed hairs, ensure that his paws are wiped clean, and that you exercise good parasite control – which as a good guardian you will of course, be conscientious about anyway.

Otherwise, it's unlikely that you will be any more likely to catch anything from him than you would be from living in close proximity with him in your house every day.

Some people have even had their lives saved by sleeping with a dog which has woken them to alert them to alarms or impending health issues. Neither will it cause your dog to become 'dominant' although if he tends to resource guard it will be sensible to have him sleep in his own bed instead.

The few studies which have been conducted on the subject have highlighted a few negatives: even a very small dog can stretch out to take up a surprisingly large amount of space, and restless pets may also disturb your own sleep.

However, you may feel that the benefits outweigh these points: letting your dog share your bed can strengthen the bond between you, and help both of you to feel safe, calm and relaxed. These can be equally important factors when it comes to getting a good night's rest.

If you prefer him to be in his own bed, having it in your bedroom can still be beneficial in helping you feel close to each other, and it means you will know if he is scared, ill, or needs to toilet during the night.

● Just as you have your own sleeping preferences, so might your pet – if you would like him to sleep on or in your bed but he doesn't want to, don't insist on it. Don't forget that just as he might disturb your sleep, the reverse may also apply!

Why does my dog circle before settling down to sleep?

The short answer is that nobody really knows, although there are many theories, most proposing that this is an ancient evolutionary trait which dogs have retained from their distant wild ancestors. It is variously suggested that the behaviour is:

• A way of checking that the chosen spot is safe, free of unwanted occupants such as insects.

• A last opportunity to look around for any potential predators who may be lurking nearby.

• A way of checking the direction of the wind so he can then settle with his nose pointing in that direction.

• Some dogs also like to dig a little as well as circling, which may be about creating either a cooler place to lie, or a warmer niche in which to curl up.

The most popular theory is that your dog is simply trying to create a cosy nest, in much the same way as you might plump up the pillows on your own bed. This hypothesis appears to be supported by an experiment carried out by psychologist Stanley Coren, who noted that dogs were more likely to circle on a soft, uneven surface than on a smoother, flatter one, suggesting that they are trying to trample it down and create a comfy place.

Many, but not all dogs circle before settling down for a snooze, so don't panic if you don't observe this behaviour in your pet, unless it is something which he used to do but has now stopped doing, as it may be due to physical discomfort. Circling round for an excessive amount of time may also warrant further investigation; as well as possibly being due to pain, it may indicate anxiety or an obsessive compulsive behaviour.

• If you have a female dog and find that she gathers stuffed toys and blankets in her sleeping area it may indicate that she is either pregnant or experiencing a phantom pregnancy.

Ultimately, your dog's choice of bed is down to his individual preferences rather than yours. If you find he is ignoring the very expensive luxury item you have bought for him in favour of lying on the cold, hard floor, don't take it personally.

Do, however, observe him carefully and consider taking him to your vet for a checkup as it is quite possible that there may be a health issue. A firmer surface may be easier to rise from if he is experiencing mobility or balance problems, for example: or a cool surface might offer relief to hot, painful joints.

6
A LITTLE EXTRA HELP

Although resolving sleeping issues can often be fairly straightforward, if you are struggling to identify the cause, you may need a little extra help.

The first course of action should be to ask your vet to give your dog a thorough physical check-up. If any health issues are discovered, treatment and medication can then be prescribed to resolve them, so that you will both be able to enjoy a restful night.

It can sometimes be difficult to find the right way forward on your own, so once you have eliminated physical health issues, do consider contacting a canine behaviourist. This may seem an extreme resort, but as we have seen, sleep is just as vital for your dog's wellbeing as food, water and exercise. A fresh eye, some new ideas and just as importantly, ongoing support as you work your way through difficulties can make all the difference in achieving a successful outcome.

Ultimately it's often money well spent, which may benefit your dog and your relationship with each other in many other areas too. However, it's important to seek help from the right quarter.

Finding the right help

With the advent of social media, many people tend to seek advice from each other. Although the general public can be well meaning, there are fundamental problems with non-professional advice. For a start, every dog is different and will need a tailored approach; one size does not fit all.

A qualified Behaviourist will be able to fully assess your dog's needs and give you up-to-date guidance based on the latest techniques and research. A fresh, professional set of eyes can also highlight what you may have missed through inexperience or simply because you are too close to the problem.

You will often see comments from dog professionals on media platforms saying they cannot advise you without seeing your dog. This is because a full history needs to be taken, your relationship observed, and the environment assessed. Additionally, your vet may need to be involved if your dog's issue is rooted in a health problem, which is often the case.

Finding the right help can seem daunting.

When you are looking for a behaviourist, look at their experience, qualifications and reviews. Do they use positive reinforcement based, fear-free methods? Are they experienced with this behaviour, and do they belong to a reputable organisation that monitors their members? The dog profession in the UK is unregulated so being a member of an organisation can give you peace of mind that you are employing the right calibre of person.

If seeking professional help, look out for the UK Dog Behaviour & Training Charter logo so you know the person is qualified, up-to-date and follows a code of ethics and conduct set by their governing body. It will also mean they will have to continually develop their knowledge and skills. Plus you have a clear route of complaint if you are dissatisfied with their professional approach or conduct.

Holistic help
Sometimes, a little additional help in the form of holistic remedies and therapies can be invaluable in supporting your dog while you are getting to the root of any issues he has. It should of course, go without saying that you should never give your dog sleeping tablets or other medication intended for human consumption. Even if the product is labelled as

being 'natural' or 'holistic' it doesn't automatically follow that it is either safe or appropriate for your pet.

We have briefly outlined below a few modalities which you may like to explore further. Although several of them can also be beneficial for physical issues, those mentioned here have been included primarily for their therapeutic effect on emotional and psychological wellbeing; in cases where a dog may be nervous, anxious, or stressed, it can interfere with the ability to relax enough to sleep well.

Do bear in mind that some of these modalities may require in-depth knowledge and experience in order to achieve the greatest measure of success.

In addition. while many holistic remedies work well and safely when used in combination with each other, there are exceptions. Essential oils for example, will lessen the effect of homeopathic remedies, some may not be safe to use where certain health conditions are present, or with veterinary prescribed medications, and some can also be dermal irritants or photoreactive. In our opinion, it is therefore safest as well as likely to be most effective if you consult a qualified practitioner in the modality you are interested in trying.

● Always read and follow the instructions on product packaging.

Adaptil

Adaptil is a synthetic copy of a natural canine pheromone produced by nursing bitches which helps to comfort and reassure their puppies. It can also help adult dogs, promoting calmness and reducing anxiety. Colourless and odourless, it has no sedative effect and can be safely used alongside medications. Although it doesn't work with all dogs, it can be very effective for many, helping them feel safe and secure, so they will be more likely to settle and sleep. It is available from vets, pet shops and online as a collar, a reusable diffuser (similar to air freshener devices) and as a spray.

The diffuser is plugged into an electrical socket and left continuously running in the room where your dog spends most time. It covers up to 50-70 square metres, and although fully functional after 24 hours, it may take seven days to begin to notice any effect, and the manufacturer suggests trying it for at least one month. Diffuser refills last for around 4 weeks before they need replacing: and for optimum effect the diffuser unit should be checked monthly and replaced every six months.

Pet Remedy
Also widely obtainable from vets, pet shops and online, Pet Remedy is available either as a spray, plug-in diffuser, wipe, or battery operated atomiser.

The formulation acts by mimicking a natural calming message from the brain called GABA which encourages relaxation, reduces anxiety and improves sleep, and many owners have reported beneficial effects.

The manufacturer's information describes it as a low dosage Valerian blend (it also contains Vetiver, Sweet Basil and Sage) but because it is based on essential oils, we would suggest that you observe the same general guidelines as for Applied Zoopharmacognosy: first see if your dog likes the smell by offering him the option of sniffing at the spray applied to your hand or a tissue, or if using the diffuser, leaving a door open so that he can either stay or leave the room if he wishes.

If he appears to be happy about it – lying down, breathing deeply, blinking his eyes or puffing his cheeks – the diffuser is probably the best option.

The manufacturers state that although Pet Remedy is gentle in its effect and safe to use in most situations, if your pet is on any medications you should consult your vet before using it.

Bach and other Flower Remedies
Individual flower remedies (not to be confused with aromatic floral sprays) can be helpful with a wide range of issues: they are also available as combinations especially formulated for use in acute emergency situations, such as accidents, shock or distress of any sort. Probably the best known of these is Bach Flower Rescue Remedy which can help take the edge off anxiety. It is not a sedative or tranquilizer, but acts to gently rebalance emotions and address negative states of mind. It can be used in conjunction with conventional as well as homeopathic and herbal remedies and is very safe to use: as far as we are aware, adverse effects have never been reported – but we would suggest that, as always, you err on the side of safety and check first with your vet before giving it to your pet.

Bach Rescue Remedy is a blend of five different flower essences: Star of Bethlehem (shock and trauma), Rock Rose (terror), Clematis (faintness), Impatiens (agitation), and Cherry Plum (loss of control). It can be bought over the counter at most high street chemists and health shops as well as online – look out for the pet-friendly version which is alcohol free.

It can be administered in a variety of different ways – but do not try and place drops directly into the mouth as this can be stressful for most dogs and runs the risk of you (or the dropper) being bitten.

Rescue Remedy and other flower remedies can be added to drinking water or food, or offered on pieces of dry bread or treats which will absorb the liquid; alternatively, place it on the top of the nose where your dog will reflexively lick it off. It can also be applied to the pads of the paws, or on the belly; or to the acupressure point which lies halfway between his ears by dropping the remedy onto the palm of your hand and then stroking it on top of his head. Choose whichever method causes least stress to your dog, and is easy and safe for you to do.

Although Rescue Remedy may be helpful, it will be generalized rather than specific to your dog. There are 38 individual Bach flower remedies and while Rescue Remedy can a good place to start as well as a useful standby to keep on hand, they are most effective when tailored specifically to your dog; as with homeopathy, the better the match the better the result, so you might like to make up your own blend.

Although Bach is probably the best known, an even wider range of flower remedies are produced by other companies; some also offer ready-made combinations using similar or additional flower essences to assist with anxiety, nervousness and sleeping issues.

There are several excellent publications which will explain more about flower remedies and how to make up your own combinations: see the Further Reading section for a few suggestions. Alternatively, you could contact a practitioner, although keep in mind that the practice of essence therapy lacks formal regulation. There are many types of certifications, and training can vary greatly. Always research the provider's other qualifications and experience and read reviews, if available. Don't hesitate to ask questions about their training, too.

Homeopathy

Pioneered and developed by Samuel Hahnemann in the eighteenth century, homeopathy is based on the principle that 'like cures like' following his discovery that substances which produced the same symptoms as an ailment, could, when given in much smaller quantities, cure it. These substances are diluted in a special process known as potentisation, and subjected to succussion (vigorous shaking) which increases the homeopathic strength even though the chemical concentration decreases.

Because homeopathy addresses the whole body, it can be effective in resolving emotional issues as well as physical problems; it is a very safe modality, and if the wrong remedy is chosen, it will simply have no effect and do no harm.

Homeopathic remedies are obtainable from chemists, health shops and online, where they are most commonly supplied as 6c or 30c 'potencies'. This refers to the dilution and succussion of the remedy – the higher the number the more times it has undergone this process and the more powerful the effect may be.

The remedies come in either liquid, pill or crystal form which need to be stored and administered correctly: the general advice is that they should not be given with food, or close to mealtimes, and should be stored away from strong smells and direct sunlight. Avoid handling them as this can also destroy their efficacy. Keep them in their original container, and if you drop a pill on the floor, discard it.

As they aren't unpleasant tasting there isn't usually a problem with giving them, although you can if necessary crush pills between two spoons into a fold of paper and tip them into your dog's mouth so they stick to his tongue. The liquid remedies can sometimes be easier to manage - you will know your dog and which form will be the simplest to give.

Allow fifteen minutes before or after eating, and at least five minutes between remedies if you are giving more than one. Simply tip into the bottle cap if giving pills or crystals (some bottles have a handy dispenser system that releases single pills into the cap), open your dog's mouth, and tip in. With liquids, place a few drops on to your dog's tongue or lips. Do not let the cap come into contact with your dog's mouth.

The success of homeopathy does rely on closely matching the right remedy (or remedies) to the individual, taking into account any physical symptoms, background, lifestyle, environment, demeanour, character, likes, dislikes, fears, diet, household and family details and responses to various external influences. Although you can try selecting and trying a few remedies yourself which you may think will be of help, if they are not working, the services of an experienced veterinary homeopathic practitioner can be invaluable in picking remedies that may be better suited.

Herbs

Herbalism is one of the most ancient forms of medicine; an appropriate herbal remedy can help to take the edge off an anxiety so may be beneficial while working through any issues your dog has, which may be interfering with his ability to relax and sleep properly.

Nowadays you will find plenty of commercial herbal preparations available online and stocked in pet stores, which aim to calm and soothe. Herbal remedies should however, always be treated with great respect and used with care; we suggest that for your pet's welfare you always err on the side of caution and consult a vet knowledgeable in the use of herbs. Just because a product is advertised as being 'natural' or 'traditional' it doesn't mean it is safe or suitable for your dog. Some may be harmful to use where certain health issues are present, and they should never be given alongside conventional drugs except under the advice of a veterinary surgeon with appropriate knowledge and experience in this area, in case they conflict with the medication or even combine with it to produce toxic doses. Care should also be exercised in using herbal preparations in conjunction with homeopathy or Applied Zoopharmacognosy.

Do not give your dog herbal preparations formulated for humans except under veterinary advice, as what is good for people isn't always good for dogs. Even where a product is labelled as being specifically for dogs, do still check and research all the ingredients and once again, consult with a vet if you have any concerns. Many of the 'calming' herbal remedies contain ingredients including skullcap, valerian, passionflower, marshmallow, chamomile, lemon balm, vervain, and lime flowers, all of which are commonly considered as being relatively safe in small doses – but we have spotted some which also contain hops, the flower cones of which are generally regarded as being toxic to dogs. Even those herbs deemed to be 'relatively safe' are not necessarily appropriate for all dogs: valerian for example, may be unsuitable for dogs who are pregnant or suffering from liver disease, and shouldn't be given prior to surgical procedures requiring anaesthesia.

It is essential only to purchase products from reputable, established companies who exercise good quality control procedures to ensure that no contamination or misidentification of the ingredients occurs. Dosage guidelines should be very carefully followed – more is not better, and can often be harmful if given in excess; there may also be cumulative effects with some herbs, making them unsuitable for long term use. Do observe your dog carefully, as with some individuals the opposite of the desired effect can occur, and he may become more hyperactive or anxious.

• You can buy various biscuits labelled as being suitable as a bedtime snack, containing herbs such as chamomile to help promote a good night's sleep. Generally, it will do no harm to try these (provided he is not sensitive to other ingredients such as gluten) and many dogs quickly learn and look forward to the evening pre-bedtime ritual. If in doubt about any of the herbal additives however, the advice to consult your vet remains the same.

'Calming' products
Various commercial non-herbal supplements, treats and chews are available which some owners have found to be helpful with nervous dogs. Containing ingredients ranging from

casein, a protein found in cow's milk, to B vitamins, magnesium and amino acids such as Tryptophan, they claim to have a calming effect and to combat the effects of stress.

Most appear to be safe to use, although as always, consult your vet before giving them to your dog, to ensure the product is suitable for him and will not interact adversely with any medication he is taking. Read carefully through all accompanying literature as some products may not be suitable for pregnant or lactating bitches, and most are not intended for long term use. While they will not directly solve any anxieties your dog has, they may be helpful when employed on a short term basis to support your dog while working through them.

Applied Zoopharmacognosy

Flower essences and essential oils should not be confused with each other, as they are prepared and used in very different ways. Essential oils can be a powerful and effective way of releasing stress and anxiety and calming and soothing.

Applied Zoopharmacognosy is not quite the same as aromatherapy, which you may be familiar with in a human context: an AZ practitioner is more akin to a herbalist who possesses an in-depth knowledge of

131

pharmacokinetics than an Aromatherapist. The essential oils are used differently with animals, employing a process of 'self-selection' whereby the most suitable oil or oils are selected by allowing your dog to do the actual choosing himself. This is done by offering him in turn those which you think are likely to be the most helpful. This is done slowly, with the open bottle held approximately 30 cm to one metre away from his nose, and his reaction to each carefully observed. It is crucial that only high quality oils, prepared especially for this purpose are used - those intended for use in burners are not suitable.

Oils should never be enforced on your dog with burners and diffusers, or applied to his body, unless he clearly indicates that he wants this. If you wish to use a burner or diffuser in your home for your own benefit, then do leave a door open so that your dog can move to another room if he wishes.

Different dogs may choose different oils for a similar issue; some may choose more than one, and they may also need the oils to be offered in a specific order, so finding the right oils can be a very individual matter. Upon being offered the oils, your dog's responses need to be carefully noted and correctly interpreted.

The process of narrowing down and then fine-tuning the most appropriate oil or oils is not always a simple procedure. Knowledge of the actions of the oils is essential: they can be *very* potent, and some may not be appropriate to use where certain health conditions are present or if your dog is pregnant or receiving any medication. They may also lessen or extinguish completely the effect of any homeopathic remedies that are being given.

If you wish to explore this fascinating modality, we suggest that you first read Caroline Ingraham's informative book *Help Your Dog Heal Itself,* which explains the whole process in more detail than there is room for here, together with details of a number of oils. Alternatively, you could arrange a consultation with an AZ practitioner, who will have a wide range of oils which your dog can select from.

Acupressure

Acupressure is an ancient Eastern healing art which has been used successfully on both humans and animals for at least four thousand years. It can be beneficial in helping to resolve injuries and health issues, and in generally maintaining good health and vitality. It can also improve the quality of sleep by relieving stress, anxiety, fear, grief and pain.

A core belief of acupressure is that an intangible energetic component called 'chi', which is responsible for life and health, circulates throughout the whole of the body along invisible but very real pathways called meridians.

If a chi energy disruption happens for some reason, it can cause a blockage (or 'stagnation') along the meridian and an imbalance can occur, which can lead to physical and psychological health issues.

Acupuncture and acupressure are both ways of clearing such blockages and enabling the harmonious flow of chi to be restored; this is achieved through stimulation of specific 'acupoints' which are located along the meridians where they run close to the surface of the body.

Acupuncture employs the use of very fine needles which are quickly inserted, while acupressure relies on the use of the hands and fingers instead to apply pressure to the acupoints. Both techniques work very effectively, but only a qualified vet can perform an acupuncture treatment.

If you would like to find out more and learn how to give acupressure treatment yourself, there are some excellent publications available.

Because there is potential for causing discomfort to your dog if you are incorrect or over-enthusiastic in your technique, we would however, recommend that you also attend a course or arrange for some first-hand tuition from a qualified animal acupressure practitioner. Alternatively, you could arrange for a qualified practitioner to give your dog an acupuncture or acupressure treatment.

Finally...

(Image©Toni Shelbourne)

Dogs don't disturb us at night because they are naughty, or attention seeking in the classic manipulative sense. Most often, it's because they are in need of something, whether that be a sense of safety because he is frightened or lonely, or because he is cold, being disturbed, or in pain. They may also need time to adapt to our circadian rhythm, while old age can present new issues.

Hopefully, this book will have given you a greater understanding of your dog's sleep patterns, some insights as to why he may be struggling to rest at night, and some helpful practical suggestions as to how to improve quality as well as quantity of sleep.

FURTHER READING

Acu-Dog: A Guide to Canine Acupressure by Amy Snow & Nancy Zidonis *(Tallgrass Publishing)*

All Wrapped up for Pets: Improving function, performance and behaviour with Tellington TTouch Body Wraps by Robyn Hood (available from https://www.xtradog.training/product/wraps-pets/ or All Wrapped Up For Pets – Cetacea Publishing in the UK and https://ttouch.ca/ in Canada)

Bach Flower Remedies for Dogs by Martin J Scott and Gael Mariani *(Findhorn Press)*

Bach Flower Remedies for Animals by Helen Graham and Gregory Vlamis *(Findhorn Press)*

Emotional Healing for Dogs: Combining Bach Flower Remedies and Behaviour Therapy by Lisa Tenzin-Dolma *(Phoenix Rising Press)*

Getting in TTouch with Your Dog: A gentle approach to influencing behaviour, health and performance by Linda Tellington-Jones *(Quiller Publishing)*

Help Your Dog Heal Itself: A-Z guide to using essential oils and herbs for hidden and common problems through the aromatic language of dogs by Caroline Ingraham *(Ingraham Trading Ltd)*

Homeopathic Care for Cats and Dogs by Don Hamilton, DVM *(North Atlantic Books)*

Real Dog Yoga by Jo-Rosie Haffenden *(The Pet Book Publishing Company)*

USEFUL CONTACTS
& RESOURCES

The references provided in this section are for informational purposes only and do not constitute endorsement of any sources or products. Readers should be aware that the websites listed in this book may change.

ACUPRESSURE
Tallgrass Animal Acupressure Resources
Details of training courses, workshops and a list of practitioners at:
animalacupressure.com
See also Further Reading

ADAPTIL
Available from vets, pet shops and online.
www.adaptil.com/uk

APPLIED ZOOPHARMACOGNOSY
Essential oils and training can be found at:
https://www.carolineingraham.com/
See also Further Reading

BACH FLOWER REMEDIES
www.bachcentre.com
https://www.bachflowerpets.com/ (US)
As well as the original Bach remedies there are other companies which produce flower remedies, and have even expanded on the original 38 remedies – for preference look for alcohol-free versions.
See also Further Reading

BODY WRAPS
www.mekuti.co.uk/bodywraps.htm (UK)
www.cetaceapublishing.com/product/wraps (UK)
https://ttouch.ca/product-category/tt-bodyw (Canada)

DOG BEDS
Wet dog mats from Jacob's Den for dogs who may leak urine in their sleep:
http://www.jacobsden.co.uk/

Orthopaedic beds for arthritic dogs
https://www.camonlineshop.com/dog-beds-mats/

HEALTHY TREATS
https://www.jrpetproducts.com
https://www.finerbynature.co.uk
https://www.meat.love/en/
https://www.ancodistributors.co.uk/Pate
These products claim to be a calming night-
time snack:
https://www.poochandmutt.co.uk/collections/
calming-foods
www.lilyskitchen.co.uk/for-
dogs/treats/organic-bedtime-biscuits-
DTBE.html

HERBALISM
British Association of Veterinary Herbalists
www.herbalvets.org.uk

HOMEOPATHY
British Association of Homeopathic Veterinary
Surgeons
www.bahvs.com
See also Further Reading

LICKIMATS
Widely available online; also look at Chase 'n
Chomp Sticky Bone Pet Chew Toy, also
available from pet shops and online.

MUSIC
Featuring the music of Through a Dogs Ear
www.icalmpet.com

PET NUTRITIONISTS
Articles on how to find a pet nutritionist:
https://thelittlecarnivore.com/en/blog/how-to-find-a-good-pet-nutritionist

https://www.zumalka.com/blogs/blog-pet-health/how-to-find-the-right-animal-nutritionist-for-you-your-pet

PET REMEDY
www.petremedy.co.uk

RELAXATION
Dr Karen L. Overall - Take A Breath
Video on taking a deep breath to relax
https://www.youtube.com/watch?v=bdffTkxqlZQ

SUPPORT GROUPS FOR CANINE COGNITIVE DYSFUNCTION
Facebook:
Canine Cognitive Dysfunction (CCD) Support Group
Dogs with Canine Dementia or Canine

Cognitive Dysfunction
CCD - Cognitive Canine Dysfunction
Websites
Dog Dementia Help and Support
https://dogdementia.com/

SUPPORT GROUPS FOR DOGS WITH NARCOLEPSY
Facebook: Dogs with Narcolepsy
https://www.facebook.com/groups/214150841
9457753

TELLINGTON TTOUCH TRAINING
For further information about Tellington TTouch, equipment (including wraps and Thundershirts), books, DVDs and links to online videos or to contact a Tellington TTouch practitioner visit the following TTouch websites. *See also Further Reading*

TTouch in Australia
https://www.ttouchaustralia.com.au/

TTouch in Austria
www.tellington.at

Tellington TTouch Canada
5435 Rochdell Road
Vernon, B.C. V1B 3E8
www.ttouch.ca
https://learn.ttouch.ca/ (online learning platform for applied TTouch courses and Practitioner training)

TTouch in China
www.ttouchchina.com

TTouch in France
www.tellington-ttouch.fr

TTouch in Germany
www.tellington-methode.de

TTouch in Italy
www.tteam.it

TTouch in Japan
www.ttouchjapan.com

TTouch in Netherlands
www.tellington-ttouch.com

TTouch in Russia
www.tellingtonttouch.ru

TTouch South Africa
https://www.ttouch.co.za/

TTouch in Switzerland
www.tellington-ttouch.ch

TTouch in UK
www.ttouchtraining.co.uk

TTouch in USA
1713 State Road 502
Santa Fe, NM 87506
www.ttouch.com

If you would like to watch the Tellington TTouches and Body Wraps being demonstrated online visit YouTube and search for 'Tellington TTouch for Dogs' and you will find plenty of video clips.

THUNDERSHIRTS
www.thundershirt.com Also widely available in the UK

TRAINING & BEHAVIOUR
The UK Dog Behaviour and Training Charter has a list of organisations who adhere to a code of ethics and conduct. The Charter's aim is to assure dog owners that its signatory

organisations and their members will adhere to the most modern, scientifically-proven, positive methodology. In addition, Charter organisations pledge to take full accountability for their members with transparent working practices, codes of conduct and (should it be necessary) robust complaints procedures. Because of this, the public can have full confidence that the professional with whom they choose to work, will not use any equipment designed to cause pain, fear or a startle response. Links to the organisations signed up to the charter can be found here https://www.dogcharter.uk/

For Behaviourists outside of the UK visit https://icbglobal.net/icb-members/

RESEARCH PAPERS ON DOGS AND SLEEP

Sleep in the dog: comparative, behavioral and translational relevance.
Róbert Bódizs, Anna Kis, Marta Gacsi and Jozsef Topál

EEG Transients in the Sigma Range During non-REM Sleep Predict Learning in Dogs
Ivaylo Borislavov Iotchev, Anna Kis, Róbert Bódizs, Gilles van Luijtelaar, Enikő Kubinyi

Differences in pre-sleep activity and sleep location are associated with variability in daytime/nighttime sleep electrophysiology in the domestic dog
Nóra Bunford, Vivien Reicher, Anna Kis, Ákos Pogány, Ferenc Gombos, Róbert Bódizs & Márta Gácsi

A functional linear modeling approach to sleep–wake cycles in dogs
Hope J. Woods, Ming Fei Li, Ujas A. Patel, B. Duncan X. Lascelles, David R. Samson & Margaret E. Gruen

Developmental features of sleep electrophysiology in family dogs

Vivien Reicher, Nóra Bunford, Anna Kis, Cecília Carreiro, Barbara Csibra, Lorraine Kratz & Márta Gácsi

The cyclic interaction between daytime behavior and the sleep behavior of laboratory dogs

Ivana Gabriela Schork, Isabele Aparecida Manzo, Marcos Roberto Beiral De Oliveira, Fernanda Vieira da Costa, Robert John Young, Cristiano Schetini de Azevedo

Sleep Duration and Behaviours: A Descriptive Analysis of a Cohort of Dogs up to 12 Months of Age

Rachel Kinsman, Sara Owczarczak-Garstecka, Rachel Casey, Toby Knowles, Séverine Tasker, Joshua Woodward, Rosa Da Costa and Jane Murray

Characterizing behavioral sleep using actigraphy in adult dogs of various ages fed once or twice daily

Brian M. Zanghi, Wendell Kerr, John Gierer, Christina de Rivera, Joseph A. Araujo, Norton W. Milgram

Sleep macrostructure is modulated by positive and negative social experience in adult pet dogs
Anna Kis, Anna Gergely, Ágoston Galambos, Judit Abdai, Ferenc Gombos, Róbert Bódizs and József Topál

The interrelated effect of sleep and learning in dogs (Canis familiaris); an EEG and behavioural study
Anna Kis, Sára Szakadát, Márta Gácsi, Enikő Kovács, Péter Simor, Csenge Torok, Ferenc Gombos, Róbert Bódizs & József Topál

Clues to the functions of mammalian sleep
Jerome M. Siegel

Playful activity post-learning improves training performance in Labrador Retriever dogs (Canis lupus familiaris)
Nadja Affenzeller, Rupert Palme, Helen Zulch

Baseline Sleep-Wake Patterns in the Pointer Dog
E A Lucas, E W Powell, O D Murphree

Development of a non-invasive polysomnography technique for dogs (Canis familiaris)
Anna Kis, Sára Szakadát, Enikő Kovács, Márta Gácsi, Péter Simor, Ferenc Gombos, József Topál, Ádám Miklósi, Róbert Bódizs

Recording of electroencephalograms and electrocardiograms during daytime sleep in trained canines: preparation of the sleeping dogs
F Yasuma, H Hayashi, K Shimokata, M Yokota, T Okada, J Kitoh

Human-Animal Co-Sleeping: An Actigraphy-Based Assessment of Dogs' Impacts on Women's Nighttime Movements
Christy L Hoffman, Matthew Browne, Bradley P Smith

Sleep-wake cycles and other night-time behaviours of the domestic dog Canis familiaris
G.J. Adams, K. G. Johnson

RESEARCH ON NARCOLEPSY

Paper on Narcolepsy in animals: Animal Models of Narcolepsy (Chen L, Brown RE, McKenna JT, Mccarley RW.) https://www.ncbi.nlm.nih.gov/pmc/articles/PMC3625934/

You can also search for narcolepsy in dogs at: https://scholar.google.com/scholar?hl=en&as_sdt=0%2C5&q=narcolepsy+in+dogs&btnG=

ABOUT THE AUTHORS

Toni Shelbourne
Animal Behaviourist, Tellington TTouch Instructor, Real Dog Yoga Instructor & Author

Toni has worked with companion animals, and domesticated and wild canids since 1989. After a long and successful career with the Guide Dogs for the Blind Association, she started her own business as a Tellington TTouch Companion Animal Practitioner. She is now a TTouch Instructor teaching in the UK and around the world.

In 2001 her skills in TTouch took Toni to the UK Wolf Conservation Trust where she met a pack of socialised wolves. She went on to work with them for over a decade as a Senior Wolf Handler and Education Officer for the organisation.

Today Toni is also a full member of The Association of INTO Dogs as a certified canine behaviourist and the International Companion Animal Network as a certified Animal Behaviourist. She teaches all over the UK and abroad, gives webinars, works with clients' one to one, and writes for national dog and cat magazines as well as writing books. Toni lives in Oxfordshire, UK.

Email:
tonijshelbourne@outlook.com
Website:
www.tonishelbourne.co.uk
Facebook:
Toni Shelbourne – Animal Behaviourist & Author

Karen Bush

Karen has written hundreds of features which have appeared in leading national publications including *Your Dog, Your Cat, Horse & Rider, Your Horse, Pony, Horse & Pony, Horse*, and over twenty books including the best-selling *The Dog Expert*. Karen currently shares her home with a rescue whippet.

Websites:
www.karenbush.jimdo.com
www.dogfriendlygardening.jimdo.com

Contact Skinny Dog Books at:
Website:
www.skinnydogbooks.jimdo.com
Facebook:
Canine books by Toni Shelbourne and Karen
Bush
and
Skinny Dog Books

Other books in the HELP! My Dog.... Book series

HELP! My Dog is Scared of Fireworks
HELP! My Dog Doesn't Travel Well in the Car
HELP! My Dog is Destroying the Garden
HELP! My Dog has Canine Compulsive
Disorder
HELP! My Dog is Scared of the Vet
Coming soon:
Help! My Dog Needs Toilet Training
HELP! My Dog Won't Stop Barking

Printed in Great Britain
by Amazon